NATURAL CRAFTS
from America's Backyards

NATURAL CRAFTS
from America's Backyards

DECORATE YOUR HOME WITH WREATHS, ARRANGEMENTS, AND WALL DECORATIONS GATHERED FROM NATURE'S HARVEST

ELLEN SPECTOR PLATT

Rodale Press, Inc.
Emmaus, Pennsylvania

Our Purpose

*"We inspire and enable people to improve
their lives and the world around them."*

Printed in the United States of America on acid-free ∞, recycled ♻
paper

On the cover (from left to right): East Market Tray, page 60; Window
Curtain, From Sea to Shining Sea, page 19; The Kansas Wreath,
page 118.

Library of Congress Cataloging-in-Publication Data

Platt, Ellen Spector.
   Natural crafts from America's backyards : decorate your home with
 wreaths, arrangements, and wall decorations gathered from nature's
 harvest / Ellen Spector Platt.
      p.   cm.
   Includes bibliographical references (p.).
   ISBN 0–87596–763–9 (alk. paper)
   1. Nature craft. 2. Decoration and ornament—Plant forms.
 3. Wreaths. 4. Flower arrangement in interior decoration.
 I. Title.
 TT857.P53 1997
 745.92—dc21   96–53570

Distributed in the book trade by St. Martin's Press

2 4 6 8 10 9 7 5 3 1   hardcover

Editor: Nancy E. Fawley
Interior Book Designers: Barbara Field, Patricia Field
Cover Designer: Patricia Field
Interior Illustrator: Jane D. Ramsey
Interior Photographers: Mitch Mandel, Kurt Wilson
Photographer's Assistant: Troy Schnyder
Copy Editor: Elizabeth Leone Barone
Photo Stylist: Ellen Spector Platt
Photography Editor: James A. Gallucci
Manufacturing Coordinator: Patrick Smith
Indexer: Nan N. Badgett
Editorial Assistance: Jen Miller, Susan L. Nickol, Jodi Rehl, Lori Schaffer

Rodale Home and Garden Books

Vice President and Editorial Director: Margaret J. Lydic
Managing Editor: Cheryl Winters-Tetreau
Art Director: Paula Jaworski
Associate Art Director: Mary Ellen Fanelli
Studio Manager: Leslie M. Keefe
Copy Director: Dolores Plikaitis
Book Manufacturing Director: Helen Clogston
Office Manager: Karen Earl-Braymer

Photo Credits: Photos on pages xiii-xv, xvi-1, 30-31, 86-87, 126-127, 166-167, 180-181 are © Ellen Spector Platt
Photos on pages 19, 32-33, 58-59, 61, 70, 130-131, 134-135, 171 by Kurt Wilson
All other photos by Mitch Mandel

Location Credits
My thanks to the following for allowing us to photograph the projects in a perfect setting:

Arnold and Dolores Delin
Barbara and Sonny Fenstermacher
Al and Beth Granger, Glasbern Inn
Toni and Max Groff
Diane and Gary Hitzemann
Meadow Lark Flower & Herb Farm
Cynthia A. Schoener, Real Estate
Bertie and Noble Smith, Hummingbird Hill

We're happy to hear from you.
For questions or comments concerning the editorial content of this book, please write to:

Rodale Press, Inc.
Book Readers' Service
33 East Minor Street
Emmaus, PA 18098

For more information about Rodale Press and the books and magazines we publish, visit our World Wide Web site at:
http://www.rodalepress.com

For Toni L. Groff
Meadow Lark Alumna

Contents

Wreaths & Wall Decorations

Arrangements & Centerpieces

Holiday Decorations

Collage Compositions

Table Decorations

Jewelry & Wearables

Acknowledgments

*I*n making the designs in this book, I had the invaluable help of growers, gatherers, and travelers in many parts of the country. My everlasting thanks go to Joan S. Mazo and the Old Broads Running Club, Eugene, Oregon; Ed Ware, Texas; Steve and Joanne Bach, Georgia; Roger Ditmer, Sea Island, Georgia; Laura and English Josey, South Carolina; Joan Steel, Hawaii; Barbara Pressler and Gladys Santee, Arizona; Frances M. White, New Mexico; Barbara Shaw, Illinois; Mary Waite, Florida; Susan Reed, Arkansas; Bob Morrison, West Virginia; Dave and Linda Platt, Massachusetts; Jenny Platt Hopkins, New Hampshire; Rose Webb, North Carolina; Mary Lee Johnson, Johnny's Selected Seeds, Maine; and from Pennsylvania: Dolores Delin, Barbie and Dave Smith, Mr. and Mrs. Chester Schwartz, Laney and Niki Karras, Steve and Michael Gaffney, Suzie McCoy, and Conard Pyle Roses.

I am immensely grateful to the editing/design/photography team at Rodale Press for keeping their work fresh and exciting. Photographer Mitch Mandel and his assistant, Troy Schnyder, and I have worked together on my four books; Trish Field has been the designer on two-and-a-half and we continually plot new book ideas that will keep us all together. It was a terrific wrench to have to leave my trusted editor, Cheryl Winters-Tetreau, because of her increased demands at Rodale, but her presence is felt throughout the book. My new editor, Nancy Fawley, is a delight to work with, and my copy editor, Liz Barone, carefully checked each and every page.

At Meadow Lark Flower and Herb Farm, when I am communing with my manuscripts, Christine Gaffney magnificently fulfills the duties of head gardener, head merchandiser, head of sales, and head finder of lost objects, ably assisted by Chad Goehring who leaves the Meadow Lark after six years to begin his college career, leaving me to wonder how I can control my groundhog population without him. In Philadelphia, at THE Flower Show and elsewhere, the magnificent Jewel Robinson takes over and is as well-known to Meadow Lark customers as I am. My thanks to all, but especially to my husband, Ben, who with his usual good grace accepts as commonplace the fact that on a given day the oven is full of sunflowers dehydrating, the toaster oven is occupied with rose heads dehydrating, the microwave has silica gel drying out, and the dining room table is strewn with beads, pods, and ribbon.

*I*ntroduction

I had no comprehension of the vastness of the United States until I had driven from coast to coast with my husband and two small children. In the days before mandatory seat belts, before seat belts in the rear, before we understood that everyone must be strapped into rigid places to save precious lives, we drove cross-country with our 2-year-old and 4-year-old rattling around the back of a Chevy station wagon. Then we did it again with our 4-, 9- and 11-year-olds, with the added bonus of a 13-year-old nephew.

We were on our way to a job in California, then back East, then to graduate school in California, and finally to settle "back home" in the East. My husband's task was to drive; mine to navigate, sing, suggest games, and plot adventures for characters in the never-ending sagas I invented. I doled out small boxes of cereal and raisins, which I rationed by the 100-miles; settled squabbles by strategic separation of warring parties, and rewarded behavior with sole possession of the "far back," a haven of pillows and quilts. I tried to convince my husband of the benefits of swapping places, and he unashamedly used flattery to keep me, literally, in my place.

We drove because it was cheaper to camp out along the way, and we needed our car wherever we were going. And we drove so we could see whatever was doing along the way. In the course of these trips and others, we managed to experience the grandeur of the National Park system from Denali in Alaska to Acadia in Maine, plus the Great Smokies, Yosemite, Yellowstone, the Grand Tetons, the Grand Canyon,

Bryce Canyon, and St. Johns in the Virgin Islands; national monuments like Jewel Cave and the Badlands in South Dakota and Bandelier in New Mexico; and some of the great state parks.

N ow I seek out gardens wherever I travel. Perhaps I hit it lucky by being in Santa Fe when the garden club runs its house and garden tour, Behind Adobe Walls. I get a more informal, but just as thrilling, tour led by a proud gardener in Boulder when I stop to admire his perennial garden of native plants and ask questions from the discreet distance of the sidewalk. In Alaska during State Fair days, I wander on a self-guided tour of the plots laid out by master gardeners.

I consult a little paperbound treasure, *The Garden Tourist*, to see what special events I can hook up with. Scanning listings by state and date, I learn at a glance when the Tour of Ponds takes place in Atlanta, when the Patio Tour is held in New Orleans, and when Peony Weekend blooms in Rochester, New York. If I hit a blank on all counts for the dates in mind, I search for a local botanical garden or arboretum. When I half-heartedly stumble upon a gem like the Minnesota Landscape Arboretum near Minneapolis, I am stunned by the collection and by the contributions of the professional staff and the 1000+ volunteers who do everything from "tipping" the hybrid roses and preparing them for the rigors of a -30°F winter to weeding the beds of annuals.

I always hope to discover an authentic farmers' market like the Saturday market in Charleston, South Carolina, where I can speak to small growers and try to wangle an invitation to visit a flower and herb farm. Through the course of any travels, even to a neighboring town, I often stroll with a plastic bag or clippers in my pocket, ready for any "flower emergency." Who was that woman on her hands and knees outside the Colonial Williamsburg Inn gathering the cones beneath the southern magnolias?

I still have the wanderlust and have managed to visit 38 of the 50 states on one pretext or another and hope to keep exploring. The variety of climate, geology, botany, and horticulture among the states is dramatic; the great state of Texas claims 10 vegetational zones within its borders (everything from high plains, rolling plains, prairie, savanna, marsh, pine woods, and mountains), while other states get between 10 and 60 inches of rain a year.

Now that I have lately come to crafting with natural materials, the impressive variety of plants, shells, nuts, fruits, herbs, flowers, foliage, pods, bark, twigs, mosses, and vegetables inspires me. If I can't grow it or gather it myself, I seek out alternative sources. Some items are available from traditional venues: Hawaiian orchids at the florist, artichokes from the supermarket, shells from the craft store. Friends and relatives ship little goody boxes of pods and

THE RANDOM PATTERNS OF TREES IN THE WILD NEAR ASPEN, COLORADO (TOP) CONTRAST WITH THE MANICURED BORDER AT THE MINNESOTA LANDSCAPE ARBORETUM (BOTTOM). BOTH SCENES STIMULATE MY CRAFTER'S IMAGINATION.

cones, or show up with hostess gifts of hornets, nests, or shells when they come for a visit. Other times I trade: my catalpa pods for her carob pods. When family and friends travel, I beseech them to bring me a little souvenir, anything natural and properly gathered of their choosing. Two friends traveling to Arizona at different times selected fig pods and jumping cholla. What treasures!

Materials from growers and professional gatherers are shipped all over the country. Crafters in New Mexico expect to purchase holiday greens from the Maine woods or from the Pacific Northwest at their local garden center. Flower arrangers in New Jersey seek out birds-of-paradise, anthurium, and orchids from Hawaii at their local florist. Dried larkspur from California, birch twigs from Colorado, and preserved southern magnolia find their way to Alaska. And individual treasures abound in your backyard.

Children especially love a hunt and will eagerly seek out empty nests, feathers, and fallen tree bark. Enlist your children, grandchildren, nieces and nephews, or borrow children from the neighborhood, to find materials for the "Nature Tower" on page 148. Approach the folks who own the larch tree whose branches you covet with a big bouquet of cut flowers from the garden. I guarantee you'll go home with the branches you need for your project. Harvest the twigs that broke off the willow tree in the last storm and stockpile them for one of the wallhangings on page 9 or the napkin rings on pages 32-33.

Since this book features designs from backyards around the country, finding certain treasures will be a challenge. Most of us yearn for what is uncommon in our area or what we can't have, but rather than bemoaning your fate, seek out look-alike substitutes. The locust tree standing forlornly by the curbside at the Fairgrounds Mall in Reading, Pennsylvania, sheds shiny mahogany pods that are the perfect substitute for Hawaiian carob pods or Kentucky coffee tree pods. While we in Pennsylvania much prefer to work with carob, crafters in Hawaii would probably rather have locust for a change. Don't have pittosporum? Use variegated andromeda (lily-of-the-valley shrub) or any other variegated shrub. Don't have a shrub? Buy a houseplant, hack off the leaves or flowers that you need, and pretend they're cut flowers from the florist. Red azalea branchlets would look lovely in the "Winter in Oregon" long boat on page 36, replacing the red nandina berries. Also, substitute materials that look different, but better, to your eye. Add a bow of gossamer ribbon where you yearn for a particular color.

There are many projects in this book devoted to backyards in a single state. You have the privilege of mixing materials from all over and basing your design on color, texture, shape, or some other theme. (I used summer travels,

TAKE A PEEK AT MY BACKYARD, WITH A 19TH-CENTURY BAKEHOUSE, WATER PUMP, AND OLD WILLOW TREE THAT SERVED AS THE MARRIAGE CANOPY FOR EACH OF MY THREE CHILDREN.

a collage from friends, and places I once lived.) In making substitutions, you will have truly created your own projects.

When you gather in the wild, it is your responsibility to know which materials are protected in which areas and to know the collecting laws in the state. If in doubt, don't collect. It's a good bet that most beach communities have laws about collecting beach grasses from the dunes, and if they don't, they probably should. Even where materials are abundant and legal to be picked, follow the rules of common sense and pick only a small portion of the material from any growing area. On private property, owners will usually give permission to pick wildflowers or leaves and even laugh that you find "those weeds" valuable. Protect yourself as you gather by guarding against ticks and poisonous plants by covering up during gathering sessions and using your favorite protective repellent.

WHITE BLEEDING HEARTS, FOLLOWED BY CORAL BELLS, BLOOM IN THE SMALL SHADE GARDEN IN MY BACKYARD. BOTH PROVIDE DELICATE PLANT MATERIAL FOR PRESSING.

While I've tried to design crafts representing different states and using natural materials from different regions of the country, this book reflects my personal travels and doesn't devote equal space to every state. My own garden in Orwigsburg, Pennsylvania (horticultural Zone 6), is heavily represented, but plants are no respecters of state lines and political boundaries. Rather, soil and water conditions, humidity, length of the growing season, and frost levels determine what grows where. And microclimates on your property, that tiny south-facing pocket by the stone wall, for example, will allow you to grow plants that are not hardy anywhere else in your garden. While goldenrod may be the state flower of Nebraska, two species bloom in profusion in my backyard in Pennsylvania.

Each project in this book includes a complete list of materials for the design in the photo. Many of the materials, even if exotic, are available to you locally through your florist, garden center, dried flower shop, or supermarket. Where I have found local suppliers who will send materials mail-order, I list them in "Sources" on page 202. (Be sure to enclose a self-addressed, stamped envelope if you expect a reply.) If you have the right climate, horticultural zone, and soil conditions, you may decide to grow especially attractive materials yourself. For mail-order seed suppliers, see "Sources" on page 202. Have a good time.

Ellen Spector Platt

Ellen Spector Platt

Wreaths & Wall Decorations

Make something new to add sizzle to a room, or embellish a favorite feature of your house, indoors or out. When you craft your own design for a wall or door, you create the precise style, size, and color for your space.

Blueberry bush in bloom in Ipswich, Massachusetts. My daughter-in-law Linda sent me the first berried branches to use in a garland.

Hot annuals from cool Minnesota. Here is a vibrant display of geraniums, verbenas, and coreopsis.

Small peppers for eating or decoration fill a market tray in front of my Pennsylvania barn.

California Wishbone

ALTHOUGH NOT NATIVE TO CALIFORNIA, *eucalyptus trees proliferate up and down the West Coast. They were originally imported from Australia for timber, but the wrong varieties were selected and the lumber warped in the drying process. The pungent aroma makes the branches a favorite for fresh and dried arrangements. The oranges, pepperberries, and pomegranates are also found in Southern California.*

GATHER YOUR MATERIALS

6 to 8 branches of fresh eucalyptus with berries, 2 to 3 feet long (Eucalyptus is available from a florist if it's not in your backyard.)
2 dried whole oranges (See "Seven Methods of Preserving Flowers and Herbs" on page 194.)
2 dried whole pomegranates
8 to 10 clusters of pink pepperberries
2 dried pomegranate slices
16-gauge wire, 2-foot length
22- or 24-gauge floral spool wire
  Ribbon bow
  Clippers
  Glue gun and glue sticks

Flower Power

Eucalyptus THERE ARE OVER 500 SPECIES OF EUCALYPTUS IN AUSTRALIA; HOWEVER, IF YOU CAN'T FIND ANY FRESH EUCALYPTUS IN YOUR NECK OF THE WOODS, YOU CAN SUBSTITUTE THE PRESERVED VARIETY FOUND AT MOST CRAFT SUPPLY STORES. IT COMES IN AN ARRAY OF COLORS THAT HAVE BEEN ADDED TO THE GLYCERIN DURING THE PROCESS OF PRESERVATION.

PUT THEM ALL TOGETHER

1 Cut the eucalyptus branches into stems 8 to 10 inches long. Reserve a thick bottom piece, approximately 12 inches long, with no leaves, or strip the branch of leaves, if necessary.

2 To make the wreath form, bend the 2-foot length of 16-gauge wire into an arch shape.

3 Fresh eucalyptus has a drooping quality. Don't try to fight it. Start at one end of the arch and tie on the spool wire. Wrap the pieces of eucalyptus to the arch with the wire, one at a time, overlapping the stems, until you reach the middle, as shown below. Tie the spool wire tightly and cut.

4 Start at the other end of the arch and repeat Step 3, wrapping pieces of eucalyptus to the wire until you reach the middle.

5 Take the stem you reserved in Step 1 and bind it to the center of the arch with the spool wire.

6 Wrap pieces of eucalyptus to the stem with the spool wire, using the method described in Step 3.

7 Attach the ribbon bow to the center of the wishbone with the spool wire, as shown in the photo on page 3.

8 Cut two 12-inch lengths of spool wire and thread each through the cracks in an orange. Wire the oranges to the swag near the bow.

9 Glue the whole pomegranates to the twigs, not the leaves, of the eucalyptus, and glue the pepperberries and pomegranate slices around the swag to add some color.

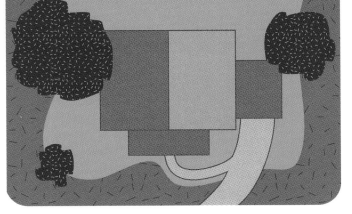

BACKYARD BITS
A Wreath Doesn't Have to Be Round

When you're ready to make a wreath, don't limit yourself to thinking in the round. And when you're making a wall decoration, don't confine your creation to a pedestrian swag. This California Wishbone is a perfect example of letting the materials guide the shape of your creation. Since fresh eucalyptus tends to droop, I went with the flow and let it arch gracefully. The more I looked at the arch, the more I thought of a wishbone.

I've made wreaths and wall decorations in all shapes and sizes, from squares and triangles to butterflies and swans. The key here is to work *with* the materials, not against them, and use your imagination! For more on wreaths, see my previous book, *The Ultimate Wreath Book*. (See "Suggested Reading" on page 201.)

Summer Ends with Sumac

IN THE FIELDS AND ROADSIDES OF THE NORTHEAST *where sumac grows, its leaves turn crimson long before a sniff of fall is in the air. The upright clusters of berries are known to produce a tasty tea, but I love them in fresh or dried designs.*

GATHER YOUR MATERIALS

For an 18-inch-diameter finished wreath

40 stems of staghorn sumac, 4 to 5 inches long

Orange and gold dried flowers (Here I used 20 stems of heliopsis and 45 stems of calendula; you can substitute dahlias, strawflowers, black-eyed Susans, or marigolds. The number of stems you need depends on the size of the flowers.)

14-gauge wire, 3-foot length

Floral spool wire

Wire cutters

Clippers

Glue gun and glue sticks

BACKYARD BITS
Sumac Varieties

The staghorn sumac shown here has velvety berries and stems. Smooth sumac is redder with more defined berries. Follow the same instructions to make a Christmas wreath with smooth sumac, changing the color of the flowers in the center to silvers like lamb's ear and artemisia, and whites like strawflowers and statice.

PUT THEM ALL TOGETHER

1 Make a circle with the 14-gauge wire and twist the ends together. This is your wreath frame.

2 Tie the spool wire to the frame. Wrap the stems of sumac to the wreath frame with the wire, with one stem pointing to the outside of the wreath and one to the inside; then wrap on a small bunch of flowers in the middle. Continue wrapping the sumac and flowers to the frame, each time covering the stems of the materials added previously.

3 When you come almost to the end of the wreath, it will become very hard to wrap on the last few pieces. Use the glue gun to affix the last stems of sumac and flowers and fill in any places that look sparse.

Herbal Wallhangings

ONCE YOU LEARN THIS SIMPLE WEAVING TECHNIQUE, *you can use twigs, reeds, or grasses to fashion unique wallhangings, place mats, and screens. The weaving is done with raffia, cord, ribbon, or wool. Here are two decorated wallhangings plus one left plain. Even undecorated, this makes an elegant piece. Thanks to Nancy Moore Bess of New York City for teaching me this versatile weaving stitch.*

Briefly Bamboo

Construct this wallhanging of dried bamboo with one row of weaving in the middle for a delicate look. Vary the length of the piece by adding more branches or vary the width by using longer branches.

GATHER YOUR MATERIALS

For a 9- by 12-inch wallhanging

33 pieces of dried bamboo, 9 inches long
3 dried peppers
3 clusters of red pepperberries
17 safflower buds on 4-inch stems
Materials listed in "Herbal Wallhangings Project Basics" on page 11
4 pieces of antique gold ribbon, ¼ inch wide, 2-foot length
Clippers
Glue gun and glue sticks

PUT THEM ALL TOGETHER

1 Follow the general instructions in "Herbal Wallhangings Project Basics" on page 11, using the bamboo and ribbon to create the base. Tie the ribbons together at the top of the wallhanging and make a bow.

2 Glue the peppers and pepperberry clusters at the top. Slip the stems of safflower into both sides of the ribbon down the length of the wallhanging. Glue the safflower in place, if desired.

FROM LEFT TO RIGHT: FLORIDA PUSSY WILLOW, FROM COAST TO COAST, AND BRIEFLY BAMBOO

From Coast to Coast

The birch twigs are from Colorado, but the herbal decorations come from backyards all over the country.

GATHER YOUR MATERIALS

For a 21- by 30-inch wallhanging

78 stems of birch, 19 to 21 inches long
16 strands of raffia
17 stems of dried safflower
40 stems of dried lavender
11 stems of dried sage
11 stems of dried lady's-mantle
11 stems of dried top onion
16 pieces of dried bee balm
14 stems of dried oregano
  6 pieces of dried red pepperberry
14 dried red peppers
28 pieces of dried love-in-a-mist
  5 dried oxeyes
  1 dried yellow rose
  Materials listed in "Herbal Wallhangings
    Project Basics" on the opposite page
  Glue gun and glue sticks

PUT THEM ALL TOGETHER

1 Follow the general instructions in "Herbal Wallhangings Project Basics" on the opposite page, using the birch stems and raffia to create the base. For this large piece I used two rows of weaving, both practically hidden by all of the herbal decoration. You can work one side and then the other, work both sides simultaneously, or borrow another pair of hands as I did here, and weave in unison with one person on each side of the piece. For this wallhanging I was assisted by Alison Hitzemann, who added a special yellow rose from her collection.

2 Try to keep the two rows of weaving straight and equidistant from the edges. Where I strayed from the straight and narrow you'll never know because the herbs hide the flaws. When you are almost to the end of the strand of raffia, knot another piece on to each side and continue weaving.

3 You can decorate using any herbs you have available, in any pleasing combination or quantity. Just about anything works here. Many of the stems will slip right into the raffia, but some must be glued on.

HERBAL WALLHANGINGS PROJECT BASICS

FOR EACH ARRANGEMENT

★ Twigs as specified in the project directions on pages 9–12 (The number and length of the twigs will determine the overall size of the finished piece.)

★ 4 pieces of braid, twine, ribbon, cord, or raffia for each row of weaving as specified in the project directions on pages 9–12 (If you are constructing a wide piece, you will want to have two or more rows of weaving.)

★ Masking tape

★ White craft glue

★ Clippers

HOW TO BEGIN

1. Knot four strands of ribbon together at one end and attach the knot to the worktable in front of you with a piece of masking tape.

2. Take two of the strands and pull them toward you, let the other two lie straight ahead on the table.

3. Put one twig on the ribbon, centered close to the knot. If you are weaving one row, be sure to keep it in the center or the piece will not hang straight.

4. Now pull the bottom ribbons up and out toward you and bring the top ribbons up and over the twig.

5. Add another twig, centered over the ribbons. Continue weaving, bringing two strands up and out and pulling the other two strands straight down over each twig. When you reach the desired length, knot the ribbon and make a bow or let the ends hang loose.

6. When you're finished, remove the masking tape. If you are weaving with twine or ribbon that is likely to fray, coat the ends with white glue that will dry clear.

7. Follow the instructions in the project directions on pages 9–12.

Florida Pussy Willow

This delicate form of pussy willow is much straighter than the varieties I grew up with and is thus much more pleasant to use in weavings.

GATHER YOUR MATERIALS

For a 22- by 12-inch wallhanging

40 twigs of pussy willow, 18 to 22 inches long

Materials listed in the "Herbal Wallhangings Project Basics" on page 11

Wool yarn, cord, twine, or braid, 3- to 4-yard length, cut into four equal lengths

18-inch leather shoelace or additional braid, cut into four equal lengths

PUT THEM ALL TOGETHER

1 Follow the general directions in the "Herbal Wallhangings Project Basics" on page 11, using the pussy willow twig and wool yarn and make two rows of weaving. Be sure to leave extra yarn at the top and bottom of each row. Wrap the leather shoelace pieces around each end and tie a knot.

2 This piece looks attractive even without extra decoration, but add herbs and flowers if you wish. For the photograph I positioned it on its side.

From the Northwest Corner

WASHINGTON STATE, *at the corner of the contiguous 48, boasts of its climate, produce, and gardens. This corner swag can adorn a doorway, window frame, mirror, or painting and celebrates the famous Washington State apple crop.*

Flower Power

Well-Rounded Plant LEMON LEAF, OR SALAL, IS A LOW-GROWING EVERGREEN SHRUB FOUND IN WOODED AREAS FROM CALIFORNIA TO ALASKA. CRAFTERS PRIZE THE PLANT FOR ITS SHINY, LEATHERLIKE LEAVES, WHILE OTHERS FAVOR ITS EDIBLE AND SWEET BERRIES. NORTHWESTERN INDIANS USED THE BERRIES AS A SWEETENER FOR OTHER FRUITS; NOWADAYS YOU CAN FIND LEMON LEAF BERRIES IN EVERYTHING FROM PIES TO WINE. WHEN DRIED, THE BERRIES CAN BE USED IN THE SAME MANNER AS RAISINS.

GATHER YOUR MATERIALS

10 stems of fresh lemon leaf, 10 to 15 inches long (Lemon leaf is available from a florist if it's not in your backyard.)

4 or 5 mossy twigs of apple wood, 16 to 20 inches long (You can substitute any type of wood and glue on bits of green and gray moss.)

2 or 3 apple "roses" (See "Backyard Bits—Making Apple 'Roses'" on the opposite page for directions.)

6 dried apple slices (See "Seven Methods of Preserving Flowers and Herbs" on page 194.)

9 or 10 small apples (Here I used 3 lady apples and 6 crab apples.)

16-gauge wire, 2-yard length

Floral spool wire

Green raffia bow

Wood picks, 3 to 5 inches long (Remove wires if there are any.)

Clippers

Glue gun and glue sticks

PUT THEM ALL TOGETHER

1 Take the piece of 16-gauge wire and bend it in half, doubling the strength of the wire. Form an upside-down L; this is the corner frame.

2 Divide the lemon leaf into two equal piles. Tie the spool wire to the frame at one end and lay a stem from the first pile along the frame with the end pointing toward the angle. Bind on tightly with the wire. Place another piece of lemon leaf on top, covering the stem of the first, and bind in place. Work up to the corner using up the stems of lemon leaf from the first pile and bind the wire off.

3 Repeat on the other side of the frame with the second pile of lemon leaf and work up to the corner.

4 Cut off four 6-inch pieces of spool wire. Use the wire to tie the mossy branches of apple wood to the corner swag on top of the leaves where they will show.

5 Attach the green raffia bow at the corner of the frame with the floral spool wire.

6 Glue on the apple "roses" near the bow. Glue the slices along the branches as desired.

7 Insert one end of a wood pick into each small apple. Put glue on the other end of each pick and insert into the branches.

Making Apple "Roses"

Each rose uses three different sizes of dried apple slices. Start with a small slice and make one cut from the edge to the center. Curl the slice around itself to make a funnel shape and secure with a drop of glue. Repeat the procedure with a medium-size apple slice. Glue the small funnel inside the larger funnel. Cut a small hole in the center of the largest slice. Put the funnel in the hole and glue in place to form the completed "rose."

Annuals from Alaska

THE SUMMER GROWING SEASON *is short in Alaska, so residents in Anchorage rush to garden centers on Memorial Day to gather their favorites. With long hours of daylight, the annuals grow to a prodigious size before the frost comes in early September. In other northern areas where summer flowers are fleeting, preserve them by waxing, then fashion a table wreath to prolong the season.*

GATHER YOUR MATERIALS

 6 large fresh marigolds
30 stems of fresh ageratum
17 stems of fresh geranium blossoms
12-inch-diameter straw wreath base
 1 block of green floral foam
 Bow made of 1½-inch-wide ribbon,
   2-yard length
 Clippers
 Glue gun and glue sticks

Flower Power

Wax in Batches

IF YOU DON'T HAVE ENOUGH BLOSSOMS TO HARVEST ON ANY ONE DAY, WAX THE FLOWERS IN BATCHES UNTIL YOU HAVE WHAT YOU NEED. WAX DRIED FLOWERS TO CREATE AN ANTIQUE EFFECT. WAXING HELPS TO PRESERVE THE COLOR INTENSITY OF DRIED FLOWERS BUT WILL DARKEN FRESH FLOWERS. EXPERIMENT WITH OTHER FLOWERS LIKE ROSES AND SNAPDRAGONS TO SEE WHICH ONES YOU LIKE BEST.

PUT THEM ALL TOGETHER

1 Cut the stems of the flowers to 1 inch. Wax all of the materials as described in "Backyard Bits—Waxing Fruit and Flowers" on page 39 and in "Seven Methods of Preserving Flowers and Herbs" on page 194. Stand them in the foam or place them on waxed paper to harden.

2 Glue the bow to the wreath, then glue the flowers around the top and sides. Glue on the largest flowers first, the marigolds here, then fill in with the others.

BACKYARD BITS
Hang Ups

"Annuals from Alaska" was designed as an inside wreath, but it can easily be adapted for hanging on a wall or inside door. Here are a few ways to do it. You can hang it on a nail or suspend it from a nail with monofilament fishing line that is tied to the back of the wreath. If the wreath is light, you can make a hook out of a floral pin. Push one pin upward into the straw base and bend what remains outside to form the hanging loop. To make a wire wreath hanger, take an 8-inch piece of 16- or 18-gauge wire and make a 3/4-inch circle in the center of it. This will be the hanging loop. Wrap each end of the wire around the wreath until you have used it up and the loop is secure. This needs to be done before you decorate the wreath base. Finally, a purchased wreath hanger is always a quick and easy way to hang a wreath.

Window Curtain, from Sea to Shining Sea

DO YOU REMEMBER LOVE BEADS *looped around the necks of flower children and beaded curtains separating rooms in lofts and pads? Updating the theme, I've designed a curtain to fit small windows that require a modicum of privacy.*

Preparing Natural "Beads"

Use only the most sturdy natural materials for the window curtain on page 19 so your natural decor will hold up to the abuse of wear. To prepare, pierce a hole in each flower or pod while it is still fresh. If the material is dry and very hard, use a small jewelry drill to drill a hole. This involves a bit more work and equipment, so it pays to think ahead. Use a jewelry drill, or other craft drill that comes with small-sized bits, for drilling holes in shells, pods, and other hard natural materials. I use a Makita brand electric drill with a $\frac{1}{16}$-, $\frac{5}{64}$-, or $\frac{3}{32}$-inch bit. Place the pod or shell on a hard surface, position the drill bit, grasp the object firmly, and drill the hole.

When I harvest strawflowers, I select as many as I think I'll need to work with this season, pierce them with a long stickpin and set them aside to dry while still on the stickpin. I can later slip them off the pin to use as "beads" whenever I need some. I follow the same rule with the acorns and nuts that I gather. Most nuts should be slow-baked in the oven at 250°F for about three hours after piercing, to prevent any surprise emergence of larvae. Reglue acorn caps if they come off during drying. Follow these same rules when preparing materials for the pinnacles on page 182.

GATHER YOUR MATERIALS

Natural objects to string as beads (Here I used dried nuts, leaves, whole fruit, fruit slices and peel, hot peppers, flowers, pods, cones, and gourds, plus eggshells and seashells, approximately 41 to 75 objects for each 32-inch strand. The number you will need depends on the length of the strand and the thickness of each object.)
Curtain rod or branch
Monofilament fishing line
Tape measure
Needle
Scissors
Electric drill with small bit (optional)

PUT THEM ALL TOGETHER

1 Measure your window. Decide how many strands you want and how long they should be. Here I used six 32-inch strands for a 42- by 26-inch window.

2 Each item must have a natural hole or opening or must be able to be pierced by a needle or drill. If you are collecting shells, look for those with holes, or be ready to drill your own. See "Backyard Bits—Preparing Natural 'Beads'," above. It's easy to thread dried cockscomb on a needle, for example, but not dried straw-flowers. If you want to use strawflowers, thread them while they're still fresh and allow for shrinkage. Most nuts must be slow-baked in an oven after piercing to kill any hidden pests.

3 If you are the precise type, lay out the items in rows on your worktable until you have the items the way you want them. If you are more of a gambler, like me, just start stringing. The bottom object of each strand should be quite sturdy.

4 For each strand, cut off a piece of fishing line about 18 inches more than the finished length you need, and thread the needle. Using a single strand of fishing line and the first row of objects you assembled in Step 3, thread your first element and tie it securely at the bottom of the line. Keep adding elements until you have reached the desired length. End your strand by tying the last item securely. Slip off the needle.

5 Repeat Step 4, threading elements onto a piece of fishing line until you have the desired number of strands.

6 When you're ready to hang the curtain, tie each strand to a curtain rod, or branch as used here, and trim any extra fishing line. Sometimes the line stretches, so you may have to retie the strands in the future.

BACKYARD BITS

Design Flexibility

Natural materials, gathered from sea to shining sea, are used as the beads in the window curtain on page 19. Only the wooden beads, the black Hawaiian kokio nut beads, and abaca ribbon are processed by the hand of man. The variety you select depends on the availability and your personal taste. Think of a curtain with strands of seashells, stones, and small bits of driftwood. Or picture a velvety curtain made entirely of multicolored cockscomb heads.

Although I didn't lay out my materials in advance, I started with a lot more than I thought I would need, to give me flexibility. I wanted to repeat themes to give the design cohesiveness but have each strand look different for visual interest. There are black kokio nuts and dried leaves on each strand, but cockscomb are on only two. Three strands have bright orange Chinese lanterns, and two have ribbon on the bottom but not the two where I strung the milkweed pods. Four strands have okra. Where I had just two items like the robin's eggshells, I put them on the same strand.

*F*ood for Thought

THE EARLIEST PEOPLES ON THE CONTINENT *honored corn as a food staple; the corn harvest is still honored in diverse ways. Think of the Nebraska Cornhuskers and the Corn Palace in Mitchell, South Dakota. We hang decorative corn on the front door at harvest time and grace autumn church altars and sukkahs with dried corn stalks. This wreath is laden with miniature corn, sunflowers, and green amaranth, representing important food crops.*

22

GATHER YOUR MATERIALS

12 pliable twigs, 30 to 44 inches long
11 dried corn leaves
 5 dried sunflower heads
 3 stems of green amaranth (This is a
   new, drooping variety from Johnny's
   Selected Seeds—you can substitute
   any wild green amaranth or green
   goldenrod. See "Sources" on
   page 202.)
4 small ears of decorative corn
Floral spool wire
Clippers
Glue gun and glue sticks

PUT THEM ALL TOGETHER

1 To make the twig wreath base, first divide the twigs by size into three piles: four long-, four short-, and four medium-size pieces of twigs.

2 Take the four longest pieces and grasp them together at the bottom. Bring the tips down to meet the bottom and wrap with spool wire to secure, as shown below. Repeat with the other two piles of twigs.

3 Arrange the loops with the tallest loop in the middle and the others on either side. Bind them together with the wire at the bottom and several other places to make the wreath stable.

4 The decorations are either glued onto the wreath base or attached with spool wire. Place the corn leaves behind the wreath and bind them to the bottom with wire.

5 Bind or glue on the sunflowers and the amaranth. Because the corn is heavy, use the spool wire to attach it to the wreath.

New England on a Summer's Day

BY THE MIDDLE OF MAY, *the blueberry and raspberry bushes of New England start pushing out their delicate blooms. In July and August, the wild berries are ripe for the picking. Between the blossoming stage and the eating stage, when the berries have swollen but are just starting to turn color, pick the berry stems to dry for wreaths and swags.*

GATHER YOUR MATERIALS

12 stems of dried blueberry
25 stems of dried raspberry (You can substitute dried pepperberries, dried bayberries, or any other type of dried berry.)
12 stems of dried lamb's ear
18 stems of dried 'Silver King' artemisia
27 stems of dried globe amaranth
25 stems of dried purple loosestrife (You can substitute dried goldenrod or any wispy flower.)
14 bachelor's buttons
8 dried zinnias
16-gauge wire, 5-yard length
Green or brown floral tape
Floral spool wire
Clippers
Glue gun and glue sticks

Flower Power

Wild Thing
WHERE PURPLE LOOSESTRIFE GROWS WILD AND WHERE IT'S LEGAL TO PICK, DO A PUBLIC SERVICE BY HARVESTING SOME TO DRY. THOUGH ITS MAGENTA COLOR BRIGHTENS THE LANDSCAPE, IT HAS INVADED PONDS AND MARSHY AREAS, CROWDING OUT NATIVE PLANTS THAT FISH AND OTHER WILDLIFE FEED ON. IN SOME STATES IT IS NOW ILLEGAL TO PLANT LOOSESTRIFE EVEN IN THE GARDEN, LEST IT ESCAPE AND DO MORE DAMAGE.

Plan Ahead

With a project such as "New England on a Summer's Day," it's easy to be too enthusiastic with materials at the start. The next thing you know, you've run out of flowers before you've worked your way around three-quarters of your wreath. Unless you have an unlimited supply from which you can borrow, it helps to plan ahead and divide your materials in half and make sure that you reach the top center of the arch without using more than your budget. Some of you (and you know who you are) may need to divide the materials in quarters to ensure that your wreath comes out even.

PUT THEM ALL TOGETHER

1 Bend the 16-gauge wire in half for strength, and wrap the 2½-yard length with floral tape to hold it together. Bend the wire into the shape you prefer. Here I made an inverted U, or rounded arch.

2 Cut the stems of all the flowers, berries, and herbs to about 4 inches and place them in separate piles on the worktable. Reserve the zinnias and bachelor's buttons.

3 Tie the spool wire to one end of the arch. Start with a small bundle (4 or 5 stems) of one material, like the loosestrife, and wrap it to the frame with the wire. The stems should point toward the middle of the frame.

4 Take a bundle of another material, like the artemisia, and place it so that the flowers cover the stems of the previous bundle. Continue wrapping the bundles to the wire in an order that's pleasing to you, until you reach the center of the arch.

5 Bind off and cut the wire. Tie the wire to the other end of the arch and begin adding small bundles of material, repeating Steps 3 through 5.

6 Glue on the showiest flowers, like the zinnias and bachelor's buttons, at the top and sides of the arch. Glue on any small bits of materials that have broken off in the process and fill in where necessary.

7 When you're done, add a small loop of wire to the back of the frame for hanging. Even after the project is completed, you can adjust its shape slightly, if desired, by carefully bending the wire frame. Here I flared out the ends after the swag was hung over the mirror.

Classic Magnolia Wreath

WITH LEAVES SO SPLENDID *on both the "right" and "wrong" sides, the southern magnolia needs little adornment other than its pods and a bow, if you're so inclined. A wreath of any shape is possible when you construct the wire form yourself.*

27

Basic Wreath Base

This wreath base and wrapping technique are adaptable to most dried and fresh materials and enable you to make a circle, oval, square, diamond, heart, or any other shape wreath, and vary the size. I prefer to use 14- or 16-gauge wire; the smaller the wreath, the thinner the wire can be.

Once you've formed the wreath base into the size and shape you desire, you can wrap the wire with floral tape. This step is only necessary when you are making an airy wreath where the wire might show through. You can make your own wreath as simple or elaborate as you wish. A large peach bow is the only adornment the "Magnolia Wreath" needs. "Summer Ends with Sumac" on page 12 is made in the same way, but that design employs additional flowers and no bow. Let your personal taste and the room's decor dictate how you decorate your wreath.

GATHER YOUR MATERIALS

20 to 24 stems of southern magnolia, 7 to 10 inches long
7 to 9 magnolia pods
Ribbon bow (optional)
14-gauge wire, 3-foot length
Floral spool wire
Clippers
Glue gun and glue sticks

PUT THEM ALL TOGETHER

1 Form the wreath base with the 14-gauge wire. Shape it into a 9- by 12-inch oval, and wrap the ends of the wire to secure.

2 Tie the spool wire to the frame. Start wrapping on the stems of magnolia, one or two at a time. Each time you add another stem, cover the stems added previously, as shown below. Pull the wire very tight as you form the wreath.

Flower Power

Southern Belle THERE IS A THEORY THAT MAGNOLIAS ARE THE ANCESTORS OF ALL OTHER FLOWERING PLANTS; IN FACT, FOSSILS RESEMBLING MAGNOLIAS HAVE BEEN DISCOVERED THAT ARE OVER 70 MILLION YEARS OLD. THE SOUTHERN MAGNOLIA IS A PARTICULAR FAVORITE AND IS ALSO THE STATE FLOWER OF BOTH MISSISSIPPI AND LOUISIANA. THIS FLOWERING EVERGREEN SHEDS ITS LEAVES IN THE SPRING AND ITS PODS IN LATE SUMMER, CAUSING SOME GARDENERS TO THINK ITS PRESENCE IN THEIR YARDS IS JUST TOO MUCH WORK. OTHERS PRIZE THE TREE FOR ITS FRAGRANT, CREAMY WHITE FLOWERS AND SHINY, GREEN LEAVES WITH A RUST UNDERSIDE. I THINK THE UNDERSIDE OF THE LEAVES IS QUITE ATTRACTIVE AND OFTEN INCORPORATE THIS "WRONG" SIDE INTO MY DESIGN.

3 Wrap on pods at the same time you are wrapping on magnolia, as shown below. The stems of the cones may be short, so for added security squirt on a dab of glue before you continue wrapping the leaves.

4 Tie on a bow with the spool wire, if you desire. In time the wreath will dry but it will continue to look lovely as the leaves curl and show their rust-colored undersides.

Arrangements & Centerpieces

An armload of fresh-picked 'Sunbright' and 'Teddy Bear' sunflowers and small white-winged everlastings are ready for the drying wires.

The perfect time to pick weeping willow is the spring, when the branches are golden and the leaves have yet to appear.

When these palm pods drop, scoop them up to make the perfect long-boat centerpiece.

I require at least one small vase of flowers or leaves in my home at all times. Whether a grand arrangement on the dining room table or a thimble full of herbs tucked into a tiny space for my eyes only, it matters not. Especially in the winter when most of the garden is asleep, the sight and smell of fresh sprigs of pine or bright winter berries can cheer the soul.

Spring in Ohio

INSTEAD OF GATHERING FROM YOUR BACKYARD, *gain double duty from plants destined for the garden. Use them first for a special table centerpiece, then plant them in the yard as frost requirements dictate. I purchased the plants used in this project in Ohio, where garden centers stock them in abundance, but they're available across the country.*

GATHER YOUR MATERIALS

2 long stems of heather, plus 6 to 8
  sprigs

8 to 12 stems of weeping willow

6 to 8 stems of cut geraniums in a
  small water jar or vase

1 pot of forced mini-daffodils, 5 to 6
  bulbs in a pot

1 pot of Johnny-jump-ups

1 pot of miniature pansies

4 pansy plants

Florida long boat, or long, narrow
  basket (See "Backyard Bits—Florida
  Long Boats" on page 34.)

Green sheet moss, dampened,
  approximately 1½ square feet

Plastic freezer wrap

1 block of green floral foam

2 strong rubber bands

Paring knife

Spoon

BACKYARD BITS
Florida Long Boats

The container that I call a long boat, shown on pages 32–39, is a discard from a palm tree found in the Florida backyard of friends of my assistant, Christine Gaffney. After a frond unfurls from its innards, the tree eventually sheds it. Since it looks similar to the long boats once carried by merchant ships, that's the name I've given it. It makes a perfect natural container for any centerpiece. If you take a trip to palm country, or know others who will, give them the commission to go scouting for a long boat. Or instead, use any long, narrow basket or typical English trug for the long boat arrangements.

PUT THEM ALL TOGETHER

1 Line the long boat or other container with plastic freezer wrap (it's heavier than the usual food plastic wrap). Cut two pieces of foam and taper the bottom of each piece to fit in the middle of the boat. Immerse the foam in water for 30 minutes and then place it in the center of the long boat.

2 Lay the two long pieces of heather at the ends of the boat, inserting the ends into the floral foam.

3 Divide the weeping willow into two piles. With each pile, bend the tips to meet the ends and secure the loop with a rubber band. Place the willow at the ends of the boat as desired, inserting the ends into the foam.

4 Nestle the jar of geraniums in the foam at the center of the boat by scooping out a place for it with a spoon.

5 Take the daffodil bulbs out of the pot and separate them. Wrap each bulb in moistened moss and place in the arrangement.

6 Take the remaining plants out of their pots and wrap their roots in the damp moss. Place the plants where desired, scooping out the foam if necessary.

7 Fill in bare spots with the sprigs of heather, inserting the ends into the foam to secure.

BACKYARD BITS
Willow Napkin Rings

Nothing could be simpler or more natural than the napkin rings shown in the photo on pages 32–33. Take four to six 18-inch-long stems of willow, tie them in a knot around a napkin, and clip off the extra-long ends. Pick the willow anytime in late winter or early spring when the stems start to yellow but the leaves have not yet emerged. Following a storm, harvest more than you need from the ground around your favorite willow tree.

Flower Power

Geranium Blossoms ALTHOUGH WE DON'T THINK OF THEM AS A CUT FLOWER BECAUSE OF THEIR SHORT STEMS, GERANIUMS HAVE A VASE LIFE OF ONE TO TWO WEEKS. ARRANGE GERANIUM BLOSSOMS CLUSTERED IN EGG CUPS OR MINIATURE BOTTLES DOWN THE LENGTH OF A TABLE FOR AN UNUSUAL BUT COLORFUL CENTERPIECE.

Winter In Oregon

TREASURES FROM MY SISTER, *Joan Mazo, in Eugene, Oregon, fill a Florida long boat. Do you get a sweater, silk scarf, jazzy knee socks, or a coveted book from your sister at the holidays? I get lichen that fell from a tree, Chinese cypress cones, camellia branches in bud, and bags of crimson nandina from my sister. UPS delivers three-day air freight at an affordable price so the materials arrive in superb condition for my December centerpiece.*

GATHER YOUR MATERIALS

   2 stems of noble fir
   2 stems of blue-berried juniper
   9 stems of camellia (You can substitute rhododendron.)
   9 stems of nandina (You can substitute holly.)
   2 stems of incense cedar
   3 stems of variegated pittosporum (This is available from a florist.)
   2 stems of mistletoe
   4 Chinese cypress cones
10 pieces of assorted lichens
   Florida long boat or long, narrow basket (See "Backyard Bits—Florida Long Boats" on page 34.)
   1 block of green floral foam
   Heavy-duty foil
   Paring knife
   Clippers

PUT THEM ALL TOGETHER

1 Cut the block of foam into thirds. With the paring knife, trim each piece to fit the container you are using. The long boat is narrow at the bottom, so I tapered the bottom of each piece of foam to fit. Immerse the foam in water for 30 minutes.

2 Make a little tray with the foil to hold the foam and catch the water drippings. Place the tray in the bottom of the container, shaping the foil to fit the long boat. Position the pieces of wet floral foam on the foil in the bottom of the container.

3 Insert the stems of fresh material into the foam, starting with the least precious. Here I used noble fir and juniper on the bottom, inserted the shiny camellia next, and clustered the red-berried nandina toward the center. I added the stems of incense cedar and the variegated pittosporum where the white tips would provide a contrast to all the green, then scattered the mistletoe, cones, and lichen on the top layer. Other pieces were tucked in as necessary to hide the foam and foil.

4 Add water every day or so, directly into the foam. Place this arrangement in a cool area out of direct sunlight, and it should last for weeks.

BACKYARD BITS
Under the Mistletoe

According to Norse mythology, a mistletoe dart killed Baldur the Beautiful, god of light. Baldur was restored to life, but the gods blamed the mistletoe. As a result, the plant hid high up in the trees and did not grow on the ground. Mistletoe is said to bring peace and happiness as long as it does not touch the ground; to this day it is usually found hanging in doorways.

Autumn in Pennsylvania

I TAKE A BASKET IN HAND ON A WARM, *sunny day in late September and search my Pennsylvania garden for the last fruits of summer. I heap the waxed gleanings in the long boat as a long-lasting reminder of the bounty of the garden.*

GATHER YOUR MATERIALS

11 stems of wild rose hips
11 stems of larger rose hips, from the garden
10 stems of flowering crabapple
12 clusters of wild pokeberries
12 clusters of Virginia creeper
8 short stems of chestnut, with 1 or 2 nuts per stem
Florida long boat or long, narrow basket (See "Backyard Bits— Florida Long Boats" on page 34.)
Clippers

PUT THEM ALL TOGETHER

1 Rinse all materials to remove dust and soil. Allow them to drain and set aside until completely dry.

2 Wax all of the materials as described at right in "Backyard Bits—Waxing Fruit and Flowers," or in "Seven Methods of Preserving Flowers and Herbs" on page 194, then pile them into the long boat.

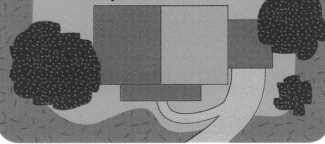

BACKYARD BITS
Waxing Fruit and Flowers

To wax fruit and flowers, you will need a box of paraffin and a double boiler. Do not put the wax directly in the pan because the paraffin is highly flammable. Make a double boiler by putting 2 to 3 inches of water in the bottom of a pan, and standing an empty coffee can or similar container in the water. Put the paraffin in the can and bring the water to a low boil, reduce the heat and simmer, allowing the wax to melt. With tongs dip each element in the wax, coating the whole piece, including the stem end. Hold the fruit over the can until the wax stops dripping, then place the pieces on a sheet of waxed paper or stand them upright on the floral foam until they harden.

Fall in Oklahoma

AUTUMN FAIRS ALL OVER THE COUNTRY *feature prize cut dahlias, each stem in its own water jar beseeching the judges for attention. In Tulsa, the Dahlia Society stages its show and sale every September. Afficionados try to outdo each other by growing plate-size, cactuslike blooms, perfect little pompons, specimens from the decorative class, or one of the astounding number of other categories. In these copper containers, two varieties of dahlias in two color ranges make a charming display.*

GATHER YOUR MATERIALS

6 to 8 stems of dahlias for each container
2 containers or vases, similar in design
Clippers
Water with plant food added, per the directions on the container

PUT THEM ALL TOGETHER

1 Strip the leaves from the bottoms of the stems and cut the dahlias to the desired height.

2 Arrange the dahlias in the two containers, as desired. Here I grouped the flowers by color. Add water daily.

Flower Power

Showy Blooms DAHLIAS HAVE A LONG LIFE AS A CUT FLOWER, BUT ARE ALSO COLORFUL WHEN DRIED. AIR-DRY POMPONS BY GROUPING THEM TOGETHER WITH A RUBBER BAND AND HANGING THEM UPSIDE DOWN. OR IF YOUR PROJECT CALLS FOR JUST THE FLOWERS, DRY THE HEADS IN A FOOD DEHYDRATOR. FOR DRYING THE LARGER DAHLIAS, PLACE THE FLOWER HEADS FACE UP ON A SCREEN OR DRY THEM IN SILICA GEL. (SEE "SEVEN METHODS OF PRESERVING FLOWERS AND HERBS" ON PAGE 194.)

Winter in Pennsylvania

Is coveting your neighbor's holly *breaking the tenth commandment? If so, I confess I am guilty. After seeing the autumn sun glint off the golden berries in the Pennsylvania garden of Selma and Barry Abeshaus, I rushed to purchase my own 'Golden Girl'. I placed the holly in vases fashioned of "white metal," an old but not particularly valuable material.*

GATHER YOUR MATERIALS

15 pieces of variegated holly, 6 to
   10 inches long
20 pieces of 'Golden Girl' holly, 8 to 15
   inches long
25 twigs of yellow-twig dogwood
2 containers or vases, similar in design
Water with plant food added, per the
   directions on the container
Clippers

PUT THEM ALL TOGETHER

1 Strip the bottom leaves off the holly
with the clippers and cut the stems
to the desired height.

2 Put the variegated holly in the small
vase and the 'Golden Girl' in the tall
vase. Add the yellow-twig dogwood to the
tall vase, interspersed among the holly.

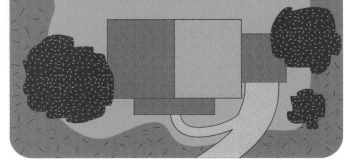

BACKYARD BITS
Trim Your Holly

Holly berries appear on last year's growth. That means that in the fall and winter 4 to 6 inches of new leaves appear at the ends of the stems beyond the berries. In order to make the berries more visible in the vase, trim off the top portion of some of the stems, and gently pull off the remaining leaves. You will now have stems of holly berries only, to place in strategic spots. Flower arranging often requires judicious pruning; reducing the amount of foliage enhances the arrangement.

$\mathcal{S}$pring among the Nation's Roses

THE MOST UNIVERSALLY BELOVED OF ALL FLOWERS *is the rose, grown in every state of the union. Gardeners from Alaska to South Texas have shown me their shrubs with great pride. The challenge is to find local cultivars best suited for the growing conditions. Here two old china containers with faded rose designs complement the delicacy of the flowers.*

GATHER YOUR MATERIALS

2 rose cultivars; 7 stems for the teapot
    and 5 stems for the small pitcher
5 stems of wild multiflora rose
2 containers or vases, similar in design
Water with plant food added, per the
    directions on the container
Clippers

PUT THEM ALL TOGETHER

1 With the clippers, strip the leaves from the bottoms of the rose stems to avoid submerging them in water.

2 Reclip the bottom of the stems under lukewarm running water. This prolongs the life of the roses.

3 Cut the stems as short as necessary and place in the vases, as desired. Add water every day.

Flower Power

Rose Varieties IN THE MILK PITCHER I USED 'PINK GROOTENDORST', A SHRUB ROSE WITH AN UPRIGHT HABIT HARDY IN ZONES 4 THROUGH 9. THE SMALL FLOWER CLUSTERS ARE USEFUL FOR SMALL ARRANGEMENTS.

THE TEAPOT FEATURES DELICATE WHITE BLOSSOMS OF WILD MULTIFLORA ROSE AND DEEP PINK 'ROYAL BONICA'. MY CATALOG SAYS THAT "CHILDREN AND ANIMALS PASS BY, NOT THROUGH," THORNY ROYAL BONICA.

'PINK GROOTENDORST' AND 'ROYAL BONICA' ARE DISEASE RESISTANT AND HARDY IN ZONES 4 THROUGH 9. THESE HORTICULTURAL ZONES STRETCH FROM MID-FLORIDA AND SOUTH TEXAS, TO SOUTHERN MONTANA, NORTH DAKOTA, AND MID-MAINE; QUITE AN ACCOMPLISHMENT FOR TWO FINE-LOOKING ROSES.

Summer on the East Coast

COOL OFF ON A STEAMING SUMMER'S *day, as Oedipuss the cat does here, with an arrangement of cobalt glass vases and pure white flowers. Queen-Anne's-lace (wild carrot), scorned by many as a weed, is nonetheless prized by others for its delicate blooms. The white lisianthus is part of the gentian family; in a vase or bridal headpiece the flower is often mistaken for a rose.*

GATHER YOUR MATERIALS

30 stems of Queen-Anne's-lace
5 stems of white lisianthus (prairie gentian)
Clippers
2 containers or vases, similar in design
Water with plant food added, per the directions on the container
Cat (optional)

Flower Power

Summer Whites QUEEN-ANNE'S-LACE, OR WILD CARROT, IS FOUND ALONG MOST DRY ROADSIDES AND WASTE PLACES THROUGHOUT THE UNITED STATES. IT IS AN ANCESTOR OF THE GARDEN CARROT AND ITS FIRST YEAR TAPROOT CAN ACTUALLY BE EATEN. I ALLOW SOME QUEEN-ANNE'S-LACE TO INHABIT THE GARDEN, TAKING CARE TO LIMIT ITS SPREAD BEFORE IT TAKES OVER. THE SIZE OF THE FLOWERS IS ENORMOUS WHEN THIS WILD SPECIES GROWS IN GOOD GARDEN SOIL WITH MINIMAL COMPETITION.

LISIANTHUS TAKES 14 TO 21 DAYS TO GERMINATE AND IS SLOW GROWING, SO I PREFER TO BUY THE SEEDLINGS OR START THE SEEDS INDOORS BY FEBRUARY. IT IS READILY AVAILABLE FROM FLORISTS AND HAS AN EXTENDED VASE LIFE IF YOU CUT OFF THE SPENT FLOWERS.

PUT THEM ALL TOGETHER

1 With the clippers, strip the leaves from the bottoms of the stems and cut both flowers as short as necessary.

2 Arrange the Queen-Anne's-lace in one vase and the lisianthus in the other. Add water daily.

3 Place the vases in a sunny window and add a sleepy cat or other favorite pet, if desired.

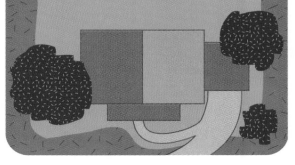

BACKYARD BITS
The Same But Different

I made the four seasonal arrangements on pages 40–47 by using two vases of a different size and shape, but similar in age and composition. Each vase holds one or two types of flowers or branches, related by species or color. Together they are more interesting than the sum of their parts.

*B*allooning in Colorado

HIGH OVER THE RED HILLS OF BOULDER, *hot-air balloons glide by, parading their colors. These "glad" balloons offer an easy but dramatic decoration for a special event or centerpiece. If you make more than one for a large affair, create a "balloon-fest" by using different color combinations for each arrangement.*

Flower Power

I'm Glad THE THOUSANDS OF CUT GLADIOLI AT THE FARMERS' MARKET ARE THE BIGGEST BARGAIN AROUND AND ARE EASILY TRANSFORMED INTO BRILLIANTLY COLORED ARRANGEMENTS. THEY ARE AN OLD-FASHIONED FLOWER, PLANTED BY SETTLERS AND FARM WOMEN IN VEGETABLE PATCHES TO BRING COLOR TO THE HOME. BECAUSE TODAY THEY'RE OFTEN INCLUDED IN TRITE FUNERAL AND CONGRATULATORY BOUQUETS, WE IGNORE THE BEAUTY OF THE FLOWERS. IF YOU CUT OFF INDIVIDUAL BLOSSOMS AND FLOAT THEM IN A BOWL OF WATER, PEOPLE SOMETIMES THINK THEY'RE ORCHIDS. IF YOU CUT OFF THE TOPS AND CLUSTER HALF STEMS IN A VASE, YOU GET ANOTHER LOOK ENTIRELY. PLANT THE CORMS IN BATCHES TWO WEEKS APART FOR BLOOMS THROUGHOUT THE SUMMER.

GATHER YOUR MATERIALS

8 stems of gladioli (Here I started with stems about 28 inches long.)
11 coneflowers (You can substitute any other short-stemmed herb or flower.)
Bucket of water with floral preservative added, per the directions on the container
Small basket without handle, approximately 6 inches wide by 4 inches high
Plastic container to fit inside the basket

3 or 4 stones to weight down the arrangement
½ brick of green floral foam
Floral spool wire, 10-inch length
Clippers
Paring knife

PUT THEM ALL TOGETHER

1 Stand all the cut flowers and herbs in the bucket of water for eight hours or overnight to condition.

2 Cut the floral foam to fit the plastic container. Soak the foam in the bucket of water for 30 minutes until saturated.

3 Place the plastic container, with the foam, into the basket. Place the stones inside, between the plastic and basket, to help weight down the arrangement.

4 Cut all the stems of the glads to the same length. Here I cut them to be 24 inches tall.

5 Insert them evenly into the foam at a 45-degree angle, with the flowers facing away from the center.

6 Have the floral spool wire available. Slowly bring up the tip of each glad to the top center, pulling up the opposite stem to meet at the center. When you have all the tips in your grasp, bind them together with the spool wire.

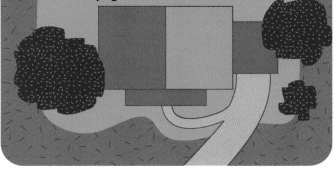

BACKYARD BITS
Up, Up, and Away

A hot-air balloon consists of the envelope or balloon, the basket (or gondola if it's made of anything other than wicker), and the propane burner. Inside the basket are propane tanks, a drag rope and tether rope for landing and launching, the passengers, and the champagne. The champagne is a tradition dating back to France during the 1700s, a time when ballooning was extremely popular. Many balloonists would land on farms, startling the farmers. They thought this strange-looking flying object was the work of the devil and they would attack the occupants of the balloons with pitchforks. To ward off an attack, the balloonists would present the champagne.

7 Fill in the bottom of the basket with the other herbs or flowers, cutting the stems short, and inserting them in the foam. Here I used coneflowers. They will hide the foam and add more color to the balloon.

8 Continue to add water to prolong the life of the arrangement; gladioli need a lot of water.

*I*nside/Out Vase of Twigs

WORKING WITH DRIED FLOWERS *allows a flexibility that you don't have with fresh materials. Use cracked antique china, wood caddies, or paper boxes to contain your dried materials. These inside/out vessels, which I've made from twigs and stems found in different areas of the country, allow you to arrange the materials on the exterior of the container.*

Scotch Broom Inside/Out

<u>The National Audubon Field Guide</u> lists Scotch broom as a "pesty shrub" found in the wild from California to Washington. In my Zone 6 garden in the East, it is a favorite—evergreen all winter and filled with masses of yellow or pink flowers in spring. I use the stems all year, fresh or dried, and the fragrant flowers for informal seasonal arrangements.

GATHER YOUR MATERIALS

30 to 35 stems of Scotch broom, 15 to 20 inches long
20 strawflowers on wire
18 stems of larkspur
Materials listed in the "Inside/Out Project Basics" on page 54 (Here I used a 3- by 5-inch cardboard box for my form.)
4 rubber bands

PUT THEM ALL TOGETHER

1 Follow the general instructions in the "Inside/Out Project Basics" on page 54.

2 To make the first braided tie, choose three of your longest Scotch broom branches. Bind them together at the stiff end with a rubber band. Braid until you reach the ends and wrap them with another rubber band.

INSIDE/OUT PROJECT BASICS

FOR EACH ARRANGEMENT

★ Small box or small cylinder such as a piece of tree branch
★ Twigs of one type as specified in the project directions on pages 52–55
★ 2 heavy rubber bands
★ Floral spool wire
★ Glue gun and glue sticks
★ Clippers

HOW TO BEGIN

1. Take the container and slip the two rubber bands over the outside, 1 inch from the top and 1 inch from the bottom.

2. Slip the twigs one by one down along the side of the container, as shown at right. They will be held in place by the rubber bands. Trim the bottom of the twigs as necessary to achieve the desired height.

3. Wrap the spool wire tightly around the twigs in two places and twist to secure. Clip off and discard the rubber bands. The wire will hold the arrangement permanently, while rubber bands often deteriorate within a year.

4. Proceed following the instructions listed in the project directions on pages 52–55.

BACKYARD BITS
More Ideas for a Vase of Twigs

Try one of these other ideas for your inside/out arrangement. You can leave the container undecorated and enjoy the colors and textures of the twigs, or if you used a hollow form, insert a small water container in the center and fill it with fresh flowers.

3 Wrap your braid around the box. Trim off the stiffest end of the braid and put the rubber band around the fresh-cut end. Now wrap and glue the ends in place at the back of the container, hiding the wire at the lower edge of the box. You will need to apply pressure to the ends until the glue sets. Cut off the rubber bands after the glue is dry.

4 Repeat Steps 1 and 2 to make the second braided tie. Position the tie on the box to cover the other wire, gluing the ends in place at the back of the container as you did in Step 3. Cut off the rubber bands when the glue is dry.

5 Slip the strawflower wires and the stems of larkspur in between the twigs, creating a design that's pleasing to you.

Fan-Tail Willow Inside/Out

Stems of fan-tail willow grow with wonderful contortions, each adding its own twist to the project.

GATHER YOUR MATERIALS

85 stems of fan-tail willow, 15 to 20 inches long (You can substitute pussy willow, cut when the buds are just beginning to break.)

3 to 5 stems of wild grass

Materials listed in the "Inside/Out Project Basics" on page 54 (Here I used a 3-inch-diameter log, about 5 inches long; you can substitute any small cylindrical-shaped box or wood block.)

Braided cord, 1-yard length

White craft glue

PUT THEM ALL TOGETHER

1 Follow the general instructions in the "Inside/Out Project Basics" on page 54.

2 Wrap the cord around the log, covering the wires. Leave the ends long but tuck them in place under the cord. This will be the front. Put a drop of glue at the ends to keep the cord from fraying.

3 Slip the stems of wild grass under the braided cord, arranging them so they are at a slant, as shown in the photo above.

Red Twig Inside/Out

The chief landscape value of red-twig plantings is evident in the winter, when the coral grows brighter as the temperature drops, and the contrast of the branches to the white snow atones for the lack of other color in the garden.

GATHER YOUR MATERIALS

90 pieces of red-twig dogwood, coral-bark maple, or a combination of the two, 15 to 20 inches long

10 stems of bearded wheat

Materials listed in the "Inside/Out Project Basics" on page 54 (Here I used a 3-inch-diameter log, 5 inches tall; you can substitute any small cylindrical-shaped box or woodblock.)

Natural cording, 3-yard length

PUT THEM ALL TOGETHER

1 Follow the general instructions in the "Inside/Out Project Basics" on page 54.

2 Wrap the cording around the log, covering the wires. Tuck the end in place under the cording.

3 Slip the stems of wheat under the cording around the entire arrangement, as desired.

North Market Tray

WHERE THE GROWING SEASON IS SHORT, *gardeners rely heavily on annuals for summer color. Starting seedlings indoors is a big part of the plan, and where gardeners don't have the space or inclination, they can buy flats or handy six-packs at the garden center. Non-gardeners have the option of treating themselves to late-summer cut flowers at a farmers' market and drying them for future use.*

GATHER YOUR MATERIALS

For a 9½- by 14-inch tray or platter

12 stems of goldenrod
10 dahlias
10 stems of evergreen (Arborvitae or cedar will dry without shedding.)
35 'Strawberry Field' globe amaranths
30 sweet gum pods or other cones
21 globe thistles
Materials listed in the "Market Tray Project Basics" at right
Clippers
Glue gun and glue sticks

PUT THEM ALL TOGETHER

1 Proceed following the general instructions in the "Market Tray Project Basics," at right.

2 Divide the tray into six sections of different sizes and make a mental note as to what you want to place where.

3 Fill the sections by inserting the stems into the foam and gluing pods and flower heads in place.

MARKET TRAY PROJECT BASICS

FOR EACH ARRANGEMENT
★ Tray or shallow basket, without a handle
★ 1 or 2 blocks of floral foam, depending on the size of the tray
★ Paring knife

HOW TO BEGIN

1. Slice the floral foam in half lengthwise and cut and trim the pieces to line the entire bottom of the tray or basket.

2. Proceed following the instructions listed in the project directions on pages 56–63.

South Market Tray

A SEMITROPICAL MARKET TRAY *from Florida displays produce from the sea, the farm, and the garden. If you're not from the Sunshine State, the neighborhood supermarket will provide many of the materials you need.*

GATHER YOUR MATERIALS

For a 13-inch square tray

25 galax leaves (You can substitute any type of moss.)

16 small shells

14 large dried orange slices (See "Seven Methods of Preserving Flowers and Herbs" on page 194.)

8 dried lemon slices

11 dried roses

12 small clusters of red pepperberries

5 whole dried lemons

6 whole limes, slit and dried

6 small tangerines, slit and dried

5 large shells

Materials listed in the "Market Tray Project Basics" on page 56.

20 to 25 floral pins

12 to 20 floral picks (Remove wire if there is any.)

Glue gun and glue sticks

Clippers

FROM LEFT TO RIGHT: SOUTH MARKET TRAY, WEST MARKET TRAY

PUT THEM ALL TOGETHER

1 Proceed following the general instructions in the "Market Tray Project Basics" on page 56.

2 Trim the stems off the galax leaves. Using the floral pins, attach the leaves to the foam, covering it completely.

3 Add the materials to the tray using the techniques that work best for the elements you're using. Here I glued the small shells and fruit slices to the leaves, inserted the roses and pepperberry clusters into the foam, and placed the large shells on top.

4 Make a sharp point at the blunt end of the floral picks with the clippers. Stick one end of the pick into the whole fruit and the other end into the foam to keep it in place. Insert the lemons, limes, and tangerines into the foam in this manner.

West Market Tray

ARRANGE MATERIALS FROM *Hawaii in pie-shaped wedges of unequal sizes. If you don't live where orchids bloom in profusion in the yard, your local florist can supply you with many varieties, as well as ti leaves and other exotic plants.*

GATHER YOUR MATERIALS

For a 12-inch diameter basket

8 carob pods (You can substitute catalpa, locust, or a similar pod.)

2 or 3 pieces of dried palm (This rugged material often falls from the tree after the fronds open; you can substitute any moss or dried banana leaves.)

3 white moth orchids, dried in silica gel (See "Seven Methods of Preserving Flowers and Herbs" on page 194.)

9 blossoms of dendrobium orchids, dried in silica gel

7 kokio nuts

Other assorted pods to fill in as needed

4 ti leaves

Materials listed in the "Market Tray Project Basics" on page 56.

Gold spray paint

8 to 10 floral pins

Glue gun and glue sticks

PUT THEM ALL TOGETHER

1 Proceed following the general instructions in the "Market Tray Project Basics" on page 56.

2 In a well-ventilated area, spray paint the carob pods gold and set them aside to dry.

3 Cover the foam with the pieces of dried palm and pin them in place with the floral pins.

4 Glue the orchids, kokio nuts, and assorted pods in place in a pattern that's pleasing to you.

5 Bend the ti leaves in half without a crease and glue the ends together. Allow the leaves to air-dry that way in a warm spot before gluing them in place on the market tray.

BACKYARD BITS

To Market, To Market

I was inspired to make these market trays while exploring local farmers' markets during my travels. No matter where in the country you live or travel to, visit these markets to find native fruits, vegetables, and flowers to form the basis for stunning displays.

East Market Tray

FROM AN EAST COAST GARDEN, gather fruits, cones, pods, and flowers for each section of the tray. Use a little gold spray paint to highlight the miniature corn or any other favorite item.

GATHER YOUR MATERIALS

For a 12- by 15-inch basket

1 miniature ear of corn
2 handfuls of Spanish moss
6 catalpa pods (You can substitute long cinnamon sticks.)
2 heads of dried hydrangea
8 dried roses
6 crabapples or lady apples (Fresh ones will have to be replaced after several weeks, or you can substitute replicas in wood, silk, or foam.)
15 white strawflowers
3 cones (You can use pine, fir, spruce, or other type of cone.)
14 starflower pods (You can substitute other pods or cones.)
6 small dried sunflowers
4 stems of dried pink cockscomb
Materials listed in the "Market Tray Project Basics" on page 56.
Gold spray paint
Clippers
Glue gun and glue sticks

PUT THEM ALL TOGETHER

1 Proceed following the general instructions in the "Market Tray Project Basics" on page 56.

2 In a well-ventilated area, spray paint the ear of miniature corn gold and set aside to dry.

3 Stretch out the handfuls of Spanish moss and place them on top of the floral foam, covering the foam completely.

4 Use the catalpa pods or cinnamon sticks to divide the basket into compartments. The size of the compartments can be adjusted to fit the types and amounts of materials you have on hand.

5 Divide the heads of hydrangea into smaller pieces and glue in place to the Spanish moss.

6 Cut the stems of the other flowers to 2 inches long. Insert them directly into the foam. The materials without stems, like the pods and corn, are simply set in the basket.

ourd Bowls

If, LIKE ME, *you're all thumbs with a carving knife and uncoordinated with a woodburning tool, use fanciful trims and braid to decorate your dried gourds. If you can wield a container of white glue or are adept with a glue gun, you can achieve stylish results. Gourds require nearly four months of warm weather and lots of sun, so northernmost gardeners may need to start seeds indoors.*

All-Purpose Bowl

It's decorative alone, in a display with other gourds, or as a container for dried flowers and grasses. Black braided trim complements the daisies and adds an eye-catching touch.

GATHER YOUR MATERIALS

  Cured birdhouse gourd, with the neck cut off (See "Backyard Bits—Drying Gourds" on page 67.)
  Dried flowers (Here I used 20 gloriosa daisies.)
  Decorative braid, 2-yard length
  1 block of floral foam
  Scissors
  Glue gun and glue sticks or white craft glue
  Paring knife

| CLOCKWISE FROM TOP LEFT: UNDECORATED DRIED GOURD WITH MOLD, ALL-PURPOSE BOWL, HANGING GOURD CONTAINER, AND STEM BOWL

PUT THEM ALL TOGETHER

1 Glue the braid to the gourd in any pleasing pattern. Here I placed the braid along the sides and bottom of the gourd, from rim to rim. With the remaining braid, I formed V shapes on the other two sides.

2 With the knife, trim the foam to fit in the container, allowing it to stand 1½ inches above the rim. Insert the stems of the flowers into the foam around the rim first, then fill in the center to create a dome shape. Glue a flower head at the base of each V.

Stem Bowl

Not every vase has to stand upright, nor does it have to come from a store. Add dried flowers to this natural container and the possibilities for display are endless.

GATHER YOUR MATERIALS

Stem end of a cured round gourd, about ⅓ of the gourd (See "Backyard Bits—Drying Gourds" on the opposite page.)
Dried flowers (Here I used 45 safflower blossoms.)
Decorative braid, 1-yard length
1 block of floral foam
Glue gun and glue sticks or white craft glue
Paring knife
Clippers

PUT THEM ALL TOGETHER

1 Measure the circumference of the rim of the gourd and cut a length of decorative braid to fit.

2 Glue the braid, pressing it firmly in place with your fingers as you attach it to the rim. Overlap and glue the ends at the back.

3 With the paring knife, cut the floral foam to size and place it in the gourd, filling the opening completely.

4 Pave the surface of the foam with the flowers. Glue the blossoms in place or insert the stems into the floral foam.

Hanging Gourd Container

Hang a gourd by itself or in groups of two or three on different lengths of braid for a mobile effect. You can use one type of flower, as I did here, or a combination of blooms for a different look.

GATHER YOUR MATERIALS

Stem end of a cured bottle gourd
   (See "Backyard Bits—Drying
   Gourds" at right.)
Dried flowers (Here I used 38 globe
   amaranths.)
Decorative braid for hanging
   (The amount depends on your needs.
   Here I used 2 different types of braid.)
1 block of floral foam
Paring knife

PUT THEM ALL TOGETHER

1 Tie the braids around the neck of the gourd. Here I used two types of braid and tied them as one.

2 With the paring knife, cut the floral foam to size and stuff it in the neck of the gourd, allowing it to stand 1 inch above the rim.

3 Insert the flower stems into the foam, hiding the foam completely. If the flowers have little or no stems, you can glue them in place.

NOTE: The "marbleized" gourd below and on page 64 in the upper left of the photo is one that got moldy naturally. I

sprayed the inside and outside of it with polyurethane to seal off the oxygen supply to the mold, hoping that the pattern would remain without the mold continuing to rot the container. I don't recommend that you try this if you have allergies.

BACKYARD BITS
Drying Gourds

Wait to harvest gourds until late in the season, when the stems have dried and shriveled. Pick them with the stems intact. Wash each gourd in soapy water with ½ cup of liquid chlorine bleach and dry with a cloth. Set the gourd in a warm, dry spot on a screen or rack to allow the air to circulate, or hang it by the stem. Wipe off any mold that forms with a cloth dipped in water with a splash of chlorine bleach added to it.

When the gourd is dried whole, the shell gets very hard. To cut into it, you will need a small saw. If I am making a container or birdhouse, I use a paring knife and cut the gourds and scoop out the seeds while they're still fresh.

As they dry, the pieces may shrink and twist into free-form shapes. Stuff them with newspaper if you want to keep the original shape, but I prefer to work with the interesting changes that sometimes occur. Large gourds, like the bird-house, bottle, and dipper gourds, have a fleshy skin that I wash off after one or two weeks to allow the hard shell to form and complete the curing process.

Winter Arrangement

A BOUNTIFUL ARRANGEMENT OF DRIED FLOWERS SEEMS *particularly appropriate during the cold winter months, when gardens outside of the sunbelt offer "slim pickins" of fresh materials. Plan ahead and harvest flowers in summer and fall for dried arrangements later on.*

BACKYARD BITS
Stuff It in a Vase

Pay attention to the container as well as to the flowers for the most successful arrangements. Some wide-mouthed containers seem to arrange themselves, requiring very little work on your part. The vase in the photo on the opposite page has two partitions to help keep the flowers in place without any extra mechanical devices like chicken wire or floral foam. The vase stands on a chest in my sunporch and is the first sight that greets the eye on entering my kitchen door. I try to have it filled year-round with fresh or dried materials. Using no more than three materials, and sometimes only one, I can have a glorious exhibit using my patented "stuff it in a vase" technique.

GATHER YOUR MATERIALS

For a large vase

> 26 stems of dried blue hydrangea
> with small to medium-size heads
> 25 stems of dried roses
> 14 stems of dried money plant
> Wide-mouthed vase
> Clippers

PUT THEM ALL TOGETHER

1 Stuff the hydrangea in the vase, cutting the stems as long or short as necessary and placing some of the larger heads toward the back of the vase.

2 Add the roses to the hydrangea, again cutting the stems as necessary. With so much hydrangea to hold them up, the rose stems don't have to reach the bottom of the vase.

3 Next, stuff in the money plant. Here the stems are very short, only 6 to 8 inches long, and are held up by the other materials.

Spring Arrangement

WHEN THE WEATHER OUTSIDE IS FRIGHTFUL, *I start longing for spring by mid-January. Hasten spring in colder climates by forcing flowering branches indoors such as an Asian-inspired arrangement of quince and Bradford pear.*

GATHER YOUR MATERIALS

For a large vase

10 branches of quince
6 branches of Bradford pear
Warm water with floral preservative
  added, per the directions on the
  container
Wide-mouthed vase
Clippers

PUT THEM ALL TOGETHER

1 Stuff in the branches of quince, then the branches of Bradford pear, cutting them as long or short as necessary.

2 Add warm water as needed. (See "Flower Power—Forcing Blossoms," at right.)

Flower Power

Forcing Blossoms SHRUBS AND FLOWERING TREES THAT HAVE BLOSSOMS THAT APPEAR BEFORE THE LEAVES ARE PRIME CANDIDATES FOR FORCING. SOME GARDENERS ADVOCATE SOAKING BRANCHES IN A TUB OF LUKEWARM WATER WHEN THEY ARE FIRST CUT TO HASTEN THE FORCING PROCESS, AND THEN MISTING THEM DAILY TO SIMULATE THE GENTLE RAINS OF SPRING. I'M GENERALLY TOO LAZY FOR THIS EXTRA WORK AND FIND THAT THE BLOSSOMS WANT TO APPEAR ANYWAY.

I SIMPLY CUT AN ARMFUL OF BRANCHES AND STICK THEM IN A VASE FILLED WITH WARM WATER. IN THE TWO TO THREE WEEKS THAT IT TAKES FOR THE BLOSSOMS TO BURST FORTH, THE BARE SILHOUETTES OF THE BRANCHES ARE LOVELY IN THEMSELVES, AND THE BRANCHES ARE AS IMPORTANT A PART OF THE ARRANGEMENT AS THE BLOSSOMS. I CUT ENOUGH TO PROVIDE COLOR, BUT NOT TOO MUCH TO DENUDE MY SHRUBS OF THEIR SPRING POTENTIAL. FORCED BLOSSOMS MAY BE SOMEWHAT PALER THAN NATURAL BLOOMERS, BUT THEY ARE HIGHLY APPRECIATED WHEN THE SNOW IS STILL PILED UP TO THE SILLS.

Summer Arrangement

'SUNBRIGHT' SUNFLOWERS ARE MY FAVORITE VARIETY for drying; they also work especially well in a fresh arrangement. They are smaller and less top-heavy than the 'Russian mammoth' sunflowers that are grown for seed, so I can just cut them and stuff them in a vase. When the petals droop and die, gently pluck them off and continue to enjoy the deep centers on their own or add some other summer bloomers like stems of butterfly bush.

GATHER YOUR MATERIALS

17 stems of 'Sunbright' sunflowers
12 stems of butterfly bush (This is
   also called summer lilac.)
Wide-mouthed vase
Clippers
Water with floral preservative added,
   per the directions on the container

PUT THEM ALL TOGETHER

1 Remove any excess leaves that would
be submerged in the vase and large
leaves near the top that would hide
the radiant suns.

2 Cut the stems to varying lengths,
as desired. Here I varied the stem
heights from 12 to 24 inches.

3 Stuff in the stems of sunflowers first,
then the stems of butterfly bush.
Add water daily or as needed.

Flower Power

Native Suns BECAUSE OF INTENSE CONSUMER INTEREST IN SUNFLOWERS, BOTH AS A CUT FLOWER AND IN THE GARDEN, SEED COMPANIES ARE DEVELOPING MORE AND MORE VARIETIES. THE LARGE SEEDS ARE EASY FOR CHILDREN TO PLANT IN THE GARDEN, AND THE PLANTS SHOOT UP ALMOST AS FAST AS THAT FAMOUS BEANSTALK. LOOK FOR OTHER VARIETIES, SUCH AS 'ITALIAN WHITE' AND 'AUTUMN VELVET' FOR CUTTING, OR 'TEDDY BEAR' FOR A FLUFFY, RADIANT SUNFLOWER.

Autumn Arrangement

THE HARVEST MOON *brings a bounty of flowers to my garden and fields. I plant the popular perennial sedum 'Autumn Joy' to watch it change from summer green to autumn pink, then to mahogany. When brilliant wildflowers volunteer themselves for duty in my border, I allow a few to remain as a foil for the sedum.*

GATHER YOUR MATERIALS

7 stems of sedum 'Autumn Joy'
8 stems of wild aster
6 large stems of goldenrod
Wide-mouthed vase
Clippers
Water with floral preservative added, per the directions on the container

PUT THEM ALL TOGETHER

1 Remove the leaves from the lower portion of the stems and cut them to the desired length.

2 Stuff the sedum, aster, and three stems of the goldenrod in the vase. Arrange as desired.

3 Remove the side branches from the remaining goldenrod and add them randomly to the arrangement. Add water as needed.

Flower Power

Multiply Your Sedum AN EFFORTLESS WAY TO PROPAGATE SEDUM IN YOUR GARDEN IS TO CUT OFF 6-INCH PIECES FROM THE TOP OF A STEM, DIG A HOLE, AND PLANT THE PIECES IN THE GROUND. NO ROOTING HORMONE AND NO PREROOTING IS NECESSARY, ONLY A LITTLE WATER IF THE SOIL SEEMS DRY. BY NEXT YEAR YOU WILL HAVE A NEW, BLOOMING PLANT FOR EACH STEM YOU PLANTED. THANKS TO THIS TIP FROM FRIEND AND FELLOW GARDENER BARBARA PRESSLER, I HAVE 20 NEW SEDUM PLANTS IN MY GARDEN. IT'S A LUCKY THING THAT I LEARNED THIS TECHNIQUE THE YEAR THAT THE COMMUNITY SNOWPLOW DUG UP MY BORDER BY THE ROAD AND THEN PELTED IT WITH SALT!

Grander Than a Dandelion

CALL THEM GOATSBEARD, *salsify*, or <u>*Tragopogon dubius*</u>. *Call them weeds, wildflowers, or sculptured puffs finer than any architect could design. Use these fantastic seed heads in arrangements or as ornaments to decorate a Christmas tree.*

GATHER YOUR MATERIALS

5 goatsbeard seed puffs
Clippers
Can of lacquer, hair spray, or sealing
    spray
Low container with pin holder (frog)
    attached, or any low bowl with a
    pin holder stuck in with floral clay
2 pressed fern leaves or other leaves
    (See "Seven Methods of Preserving
    Flowers and Herbs" on page 194.)
2 chopsticks (optional)

PUT THEM ALL TOGETHER

1 Cut and spray the goatsbeard as described in "Backyard Bits—Preserving Puffs" at right. Stand them in a jar or coffee can to dry without letting the puffs touch each other.

2 Cut the stems to different lengths. Here they range from 5 to 15 inches. Insert them in the pin holder at different angles, as shown in the photo at left.

3 Place the leaves at the base of the stems, hiding the pin holder. Add chopsticks for a decorative element, if desired.

BACKYARD BITS
Preserving Puffs

While I had to purchase seeds to grow these "weeds" in my Pennsylvania garden, my Audubon guide says goatsbeard grows throughout the country in vacant lots, roadsides, and fields. Like dandelion puffs, the seeds are quick to parachute away at the slightest breeze. You must gather them the first day they open and coat with a lacquer spray before you cut them or immediately thereafter.

How do you know it's the first day they open? If you plant them in your garden, it's easy—watch them daily. In the wild there are plenty; those that are older will tell you so by shattering when you try to pick them. Or, pick the spent blossoms before they puff out and stand them in a can or jar. Most will continue to mature as they are drying and puff out in your home within 3 to 5 days of picking. Some won't. *C'est la vie.*

To preserve puffs, spray a light coat of lacquer around each puff, let dry for a minute, then store upright in a jar until ready to use. Start by spraying from a distance of 18 inches from the puffs, gradually moving to about 8 inches away, so the force of the spray doesn't disperse the seeds. Harvest and spray dandelion puffs in a similar way except hang them upside down rather than stand them in a jar.

Umbrella Topiaries

JAPANESE GARDENS, LIKE THOSE IN SAN FRANCISCO'S GOLDEN GATE *Park, Brooklyn's Botanic Garden, Minnesota's Landscape Arboretum, and San Antonio's Brackenridge Park, attract visitors like a magnet. Using half a ball to produce umbrella-shaped topiaries and copies of old Japanese baskets for the containers help to enhance the Asian flavor of these designs.*

Larkspur Topiary

Delicate pink blooms of the dried larkspur remind me of the Japanese weeping cherries I climbed on as a child, pretending I was in fairyland. A gift of the Japanese Government to the City of Philadelphia many decades ago, the trees still bloom in Fairmount Park.

GATHER YOUR MATERIALS

30 love-in-a-mist seed pods (You can substitute small strawflowers or other flowers.)
24 stems of larkspur
6 stems of oats or other grain
6 pieces of pressed fern (See "Seven Methods of Preserving Flowers and Herbs" on page 194.)
30 stems of wheat
Glue gun and glue sticks
Floral pins
Green sheet moss
Material listed in the "Umbrella Topiary Project Basics" on page 80

PUT THEM ALL TOGETHER

1 Follow the general instructions in the "Umbrella Topiary Project Basics" on page 80.

2 Glue the love-in-a-mist seed pods in place at the top center of the topiary.

3 Cut the stems of the larkspur so you have 6 to 7 inches of flowers remaining. Glue and/or pin them to the topiary in six even sections. Allow some to droop down below the cut ball, as shown in the photo at right.

4 In the six spaces between the larkspur, glue and/or pin the oats, fern, and wheat.

5 Finish by covering the floral foam in the basket with a layer of the sheet moss.

FROM LEFT TO RIGHT: FROM THE CITY STREETS, LARKSPUR TOPIARY

UMBRELLA TOPIARY PROJECT BASICS

FOR EACH ARRANGEMENT

★ Styrofoam ball, 6 to 8 inches in diameter
★ Stick, straight or curved, 18 to 24 inches tall (You can always cut this shorter later.)
★ Basket or other container without a handle
★ 2 to 3 handfuls of stones
★ 1 or 2 bricks of brown floral foam or Styrofoam, depending on the size of the basket
★ Green sheet moss, about 24 inches square
★ 12 to 15 floral pins
★ Lazy Susan (optional)
★ Serrated bread knife
★ Clippers
★ Glue gun and glue sticks

HOW TO BEGIN

1. Cut a foam block or blocks to fit tightly into the basket or container. Fill the rest of the basket around the edges with stones to weight down the basket and to balance the topiary when it's completed.

2. Slice the Styrofoam ball in half with the serrated knife. Cover one of the halves with the green sheet moss, using floral pins and/or glue to affix the moss to the ball. Cover both the round surface and the cut surface, which will form the underside of the umbrella. Keep the other half of the Styrofoam ball for another project.

3. Judge how long you want the stick, the trunk of the topiary, to be and cut it shorter, if desired. A good rule of thumb to follow is the height of the topiary should be twice the diameter of the container.

4. Cut a point at each end of the stick. Place one end in the foam in the basket and the other end in the center of the flat side of the moss-covered ball.

5. Place the basket on the lazy Susan to make it easier to decorate, if desired. Proceed following the instructions listed in the project directions on pages 78–81.

From the City Streets

The great cities of the Northeast offer a wealth of materials along their streets. Sumac, known as a weed tree, offers the first tinges of red in the late summer. Maples turn a brilliant yellow. Catch the ginkgos earlier to capture the intense green of the leaves.

GATHER YOUR MATERIALS

10 pressed green ginkgo leaves (See "Seven Methods of Preserving Flowers and Herbs" on page 194.)
8 pressed yellow maple leaves
24 pressed red sumac leaves
1 or 2 cicada shells (optional)
Glue gun and glue sticks
Floral pins
Green sheet moss
Materials listed in the "Umbrella Topiary Project Basics" on the opposite page

BACKYARD BITS
Gathering in the City

Gathering along the city streets means both respecting private property and public spaces. Be on the lookout for leaves and pods that fall to the ground. You'll need to act fast to collect fallen branches because street sweepers quickly dispatch them after storms.

PUT THEM ALL TOGETHER

1 Follow the general instructions in the "Umbrella Topiary Project Basics" on the opposite page. Here I used a side branch of contorted hazel (also known as Harry Lauder's Walking Stick) with the catkins attached, for the trunk.

2 Glue on the red sumac leaves first in an even pattern around the lower edge of the topiary. Allow the leaves to droop below the cut edge of the ball.

3 Glue or pin on the next row of leaves; I used the yellow maple here. Lastly, attach the ginkgo leaves at the top center of the topiary.

4 Cover the floral foam in the basket with a layer of sheet moss. Glue the cicadas to a tree branch, if desired.

$\mathcal{A}$ Tisket, a Tasket

USE WHATEVER MATERIALS YOU HAVE IN ABUNDANCE *to form a simple basket. Hang it from a peg on the wall or place it on a table. Display it by itself or with the addition of other flowers.*

Minnesota Gayfeather Basket

Several species of gayfeather grow wild on the Minnesota prairie (and may be protected), but cultivated varieties are becoming popular in perennial gardens throughout the state and elsewhere. Gayfeather air-dries easily, retaining its robust lilac color.

GATHER YOUR MATERIALS

For a basket 16 inches tall and 5 inches in diameter

> 50 stems of dried gayfeather (This is available from a florist.)
> 10 to 20 strands of purple or natural-colored raffia
> Strong rubber band
> Clippers
> Scissors

FROM LEFT TO RIGHT: NEBRASKA GOLDENROD BASKET, MAINE ARTEMISIA BASKET, AND MINNESOTA GAYFEATHER BASKET

PUT THEM ALL TOGETHER

1 Reserve six stems of gayfeather and set them aside. Cut the other pieces into 5-inch lengths, starting from the top and working down. You will probably get two or three pieces from each stem. Discard the small bits.

2 Bunch the cut pieces in your hand, with all the lilac at the top, intermingling the pieces with less color. When you have gathered as much as you can hold, slip a rubber band over the bundle.

3 Gently slide the other pieces under the rubber band until you have included all of the 5-inch pieces.

4 Take the reserved pieces. Cut four of them to 16 inches. Insert them on opposite sides of the rubber band.

5 Have the raffia handy. Cut the last two pieces of gayfeather to 12 inches. Put them between the uprights and bind them with a piece of raffia.

6 Place the rest of the raffia over the rubber band and tie in a knot. Cut the raffia ends to 2 inches.

Nebraska Goldenrod Basket

The Nebraska state flower carpets the fields in fall with blazing golden color as it does in states from Maine to Florida, across Texas to California, and throughout much of Canada. Goldenrod is also the state flower of Kentucky. It shouldn't be too hard to gather enough stems of this flower to make this basket.

GATHER YOUR MATERIALS

For a basket 15 inches tall and 5 inches in diameter

A big armful of goldenrod, cut before the flowers are fully open
2 strong rubber bands
8-inch piece of floral spool wire or other thin wire
Ribbon, 1-yard length
Clippers
Scissors

PUT THEM ALL TOGETHER

1 Hang the goldenrod in bunches to air-dry. See "Seven Methods of Preserving Flowers and Herbs" on page 194.

2 When dry, cut the stems in 8-inch pieces, reserving four 24-inch stems for the handle.

3 Bunch the cut pieces in your hand, with the golden flowers at the top. When you can't hold any more, slip two rubber bands over the bundle, one near the top and one near the bottom. Gently slide the other pieces under the rubber bands, until the bundle is as wide as you want it to be.

4 Take the reserved 24-inch stems and slip two stems under the rubber bands on the left of the bundle and two stems directly opposite on the right. Take the tops, gently cross them, and bind together about 5 to 6 inches down from the top with the wire.

5 Cut the ribbon into two ½-yard lengths. Tie one length over each rubber band, forming a bow.

Maine Artemisia Basket

Artemisia grows wild along the rocky Maine coast. Its sweet/pungent aroma mixes with the salty air to produce a scent that's found nowhere else. To protect the coastline and save yourself a trip to Maine, pick artemisia from your garden or purchase it dried to make this fragrant basket.

GATHER YOUR MATERIALS

For a basket 15 inches tall and 7 inches in diameter

Armful of 'Silver King' artemisia
1½ yards of ribbon
2 strong rubber bands
Clippers
Scissors
20 rosebuds on stems, or other
    flowers (optional)

PUT THEM ALL TOGETHER

1 Hang the artemisia in bunches to air-dry. See "Seven Methods of Preserving Flowers and Herbs" on page 194.

2 When dry, cut stems into 5-inch pieces, reserving four 24-inch stems for the handle.

3 Gather a handful of cut pieces and slip the rubber bands over the bundle, one near the top and one near the bottom. Gently slide the other pieces under the rubber bands until the bundle is as wide as you want it to be.

4 Take the reserved 24-inch stems and slip two stems under the rubber bands on the left of the bundle and two stems directly opposite on the right. Take the tops, gently cross them, and bind about 5 to 6 inches down from the top with the wire.

5 Cut the rose or other flower stems to 2 inches and insert them in the basket, if desired, leaving a border of the artemisia all around. The compact artemisia will hold the flower stems without any other device.

6 Cut the ribbon into two lengths of 18 inches and one length of 12 inches. Tie the longer pieces in a bow around each rubber band. Tie a ribbon bow with the shorter length where the stems cross to make the handle.

Holiday Decorations

Whether they are magnificent mantel displays, fanciful wreaths, or long-lasting topiary trees, natural crafts make holiday decorating satisfying. A holiday glow begins from the time you start planning your designs and gathering materials. You may even decide to grow certain plants specifically for a special event. Your designs will be unique because of the available materials you work with and the personal touches you add.

Bright dahlias in a New York garden are at a perfect color and stage for drying.

Exotic but close to home, Pennsylvania rheas produce huge eggs for my Easter mantel.

Gourds at Sculps Hill Herb Farm in Auburn, Pennsylvania, do more than decorate the garden; birds return here yearly to nest.

*T*hanksgiving Harvest Mantel

IN OCTOBER, *construct a mantel celebrating the harvest and keep it for Halloween, through Thanksgiving, and until you're ready to put up your Christmas decorations. You may have to replace the pumpkins, but the other materials are dried or will dry in place.*

GATHER YOUR MATERIALS

For a 6½-foot-long mantel

    5 stems of hops vines, 3 feet long
    3 stems of cotoneaster
   14 stems of lion's-ear
   16 stems of hydrangea
   14 stems of tall red amaranth
   10 stems of love-lies-bleeding
    7 pumpkins, squash, or gourds
   Materials listed in the "Mantel Medleys
      Project Basics" on page 92
    3 picture frames
   Purchased cornucopia

PUT THEM ALL TOGETHER

1 Follow the general directions in "Mantel Medleys Project Basics" on page 92.

2 Prop the frames on the mantel and drape or wrap the vines around them. If you have a mirror or picture above the mantel, you can use that instead.

3 Insert the stems of cotoneaster into the wet floral foam. They will dry in place.

4 Insert the other tall materials—the lion's-ear, hydrangea, and red amaranth—into the foam, positioning them where desired.

5 Place the cornucopia on the mantel and fill with a bunch of love-lies-bleeding.

6 Position the pumpkins, squash, or gourds. Fill in with the other materials, letting the love-lies-bleeding drape downward, the way it grows.

Flower Power

An Unusual Flower LION'S-EAR (LEONOTIS LEONURUS) IS A SPECTACULAR ANNUAL FOR THE BACK OF THE BORDER AND A LONG-LASTING CUT FLOWER. HARVEST IT FOR DRYING WHEN TWO OR THREE OF THE BALLS ARE IN BLOOM, AND HANG IT UPSIDE DOWN UNTIL THE WHOLE STEM IS THOROUGHLY STIFF.

Christmas Gleaming

GILDED GOURDS AND ARTICHOKES *cast a warm glow over corn, cones, and other dried materials from the garden in this long-lasting holiday construction.*

GATHER YOUR MATERIALS

For a 6½-foot-long mantel

3 dried artichokes (See "Seven Methods of Preserving Flowers and Herbs" on page 194.)

3 dried birdhouse gourds

3 dried gooseneck gourds

3 dried 'Turk's turban' gourds

3 small ears of dried decorative corn

4 dried sunflower heads with or without seeds

10 to 15 stems of fresh pine to fill in as needed

2 dried okra pods

2 large pinecones

3 dried pomegranates

11 ears of dried strawberry corn

2 additional handfuls of green sheet moss

Materials listed in "Mantel Medleys Project Basics" on page 92

6-inch-tall plant stand

Sun-shaped or other large ornament

Gold spray paint

Copper spray paint

Gold mesh ribbon, 8-foot length

Floral spool wire

Clippers

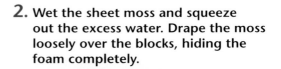

MANTEL MEDLEYS PROJECT BASICS

FOR EACH ARRANGEMENT
(excluding the Easter/Spring Mantel)

★ 3 or 4 whole blocks of green floral foam
★ 3 or 4 floral foam trays, depending on the size of your mantel
★ Green sheet moss to cover blocks of foam
★ Clippers

HOW TO BEGIN

1. Saturate the blocks of floral foam with water and place them each in a foam tray. For projects using dried or preserved materials, skip this step and begin with Step 2. If you are making the "Easter/Spring Mantel," skip these instructions and go straight to the project directions on page 99.

2. Wet the sheet moss and squeeze out the excess water. Drape the moss loosely over the blocks, hiding the foam completely.

3. Proceed following the instructions listed in the project directions on pages 88–101.

4. If you are using live materials in your arrangement, add water to the foam blocks every day to keep the materials fresh. Foliage will last at least two to three weeks this way. Fresh flowers may have to be replaced in a week or substitute them with dried flowers.

PUT THEM ALL TOGETHER

1 Follow the general instructions in "Mantel Medleys Project Basics," above. Place the trays of foam blocks at intervals along the mantel.

2 In a well-ventilated place, spray paint the artichokes copper and the gourds and decorative corn gold, copper, or a combination of the two and set them aside to dry.

Spray Painting Dried Materials

Most of the dried materials in the "Christmas Gleaming" mantel project on pages 90–93 are spray painted gold, copper, or a combination of the two colors; only the sunflower seed heads, the strawberry corn, and the pomegranates are left unpainted. Sometimes I start with gold paint then add a light coat of copper; sometimes I do the reverse. Experiment with your own color combinations using gold and copper or your own selection. If you're not feeling adventurous, stick with one color per item. Play with the paint and have a good time, but wear gloves, spray outdoors or in a well-ventilated area, and stay upwind of the fumes at all times.

3 Put the plant stand near the center of the mantel and place the sun or other ornament on it. Drape the additional moss over the stand to hide it.

4 Place the largest gourds along the mantel first. Position some upright and others at odd angles.

5 Work with the next largest materials, the sunflower heads, and insert them into the foam blocks.

6 Push the pine into the wet foam, some vertically and some draping down over the mantel.

7 Scatter the remaining materials along the mantel. For items that don't want to stay in place, cut some pieces of spool wire, and attach them to a branch of pine or other stable element. In this conglomeration of materials, use what you have and put it where it fits in.

Christmas Preserved

THIS FIREPLACE *gets regular use throughout the winter, so I made sure the materials I chose for the mantel decorations could withstand the heat.*

GATHER YOUR MATERIALS

For a 6½-foot-long mantel

13 dried hydrangea heads

5 large pinecones

4 stems of preserved magnolia, about 2 feet long

14 stems of fresh arborvitae (You can substitute preserved arborvitae or juniper, or fresh boxwood.)

12 stems of money plant, 6 to 15 inches long

25 stems of rose hips, 8 to 12 inches long

4 branches of wild rose hips, about 4 feet long

Materials listed in "Mantel Medleys Project Basics" on page 92

Gold spray paint

Clippers

Floral spool wire

PUT THEM ALL TOGETHER

1 Follow the general directions in "Mantel Medleys Project Basics" on page 92. If you are using all dried and preserved materials, do not wet the floral foam.

2 Place the trays at the two ends of the mantel. Use the spool wire to wrap the containers to the mantel; they may get top-heavy when the tall stems are added. I was able to slip the wire through a crack

between the mantel and wall, bringing it around and tying each container in place. Use your ingenuity with the mantel you are working with. If there is no way to wrap them, weight down the containers with some stones gathered from your garden.

3 In a well-ventilated area, spray paint the hydrangea heads and pinecones gold and set them aside to dry.

4 With the clippers trim the side branches and excess leaves (where they are overlapping and hiding each other) from the magnolia stems and reserve.

5 Work on both sides of the mantel simultaneously, dividing up the material as you go. Here I was working to highlight an oil painting attributed to the grandmother of the inn's owner so I formed two related L-shaped designs on each side of the painting. They are loosely balanced but not identical.

6 Stand the two tallest stems of magnolia in the foam in the trays on each side of the mantel. Insert the remaining two pieces horizontally to form an L. On the opposite side of the mantel will be an inverted L.

7 Fill in with the fresh arborvitae. If you are using fresh foliage, be sure the stems go into the wet foam.

8 Now add the hydrangea heads, stems of money plant and rose hips, and the reserved magnolia leaves, keeping the two arrangements balanced. Place the cones where they will be visible.

9 Finally, drape the long branches of rose hips in the front. You will probably need some pieces of floral wire to attach them to the mantel or weighted container.

*W*inter Solstice Mantel

ON THE SHORTEST DAY OF THE YEAR, *the winter solstice celebration brings promise that spring will reappear. The sights and scents of fresh evergreens, herbs, and flowering bulbs drive away dismay at the long winter to come.*

GATHER YOUR MATERIALS

For a 6-foot-long mantel

3 flowering white kale (You can substitute fresh or dried white hydrangea heads.)

9 branchlets of holly or other berried shrub (3 per block of floral foam)

10 or more stems each of pine and gray santolina to fill in as needed (You can substitute rosemary, artemisia, or other herb.)

2 pots of forced amaryllis
2 pots of forced narcissus (Here I've used 5 bulbs in one pot, 6 in the other.)
4 additional narcissus bulbs, just sprouting
Materials listed in "Mantel Medleys Project Basics" on page 92
5 candle prongs
5 candle tapers, 14 inches long
6 shiny glass ornaments
5 small clay pots

PUT THEM ALL TOGETHER

1 Follow the general instructions in "Mantel Medleys Project Basics" on page 92.

2 Cut the kale and trim off the bottom leaves. Let the kale stand in water for at least eight hours to condition. Do the same to the holly, pine, and santolina.

3 Place the pots of forced amaryllis and narcissus, along with the trays of foam, on the mantel. Insert the candle prongs into the foam and position the candle tapers.

Flower Power

Forcing Bulbs NARCISSUS ARE THE EASIEST BULBS TO FORCE. PURCHASE THEM IN THE FALL FROM CATALOGS OR GARDEN CENTERS. PUT THE BULBS IN A SHALLOW BOWL, ADD WATER TO COVER THE BOTTOM OF THEM, AND PUT THE BOWL NEAR A BRIGHT WINDOW. PUT PEBBLES IN THE BOTTOM OF THE DISH TO HELP KEEP THE BULBS UPRIGHT AS THE ROOTS GROW. WHEN I WEDGE FOUR TO SIX BULBS IN THE BOWL, I USUALLY OMIT THE PEBBLES BECAUSE THE BULBS SUPPORT EACH OTHER. ADD A SMALL AMOUNT OF WATER EVERY FEW DAYS TO KEEP THE ROOTS WET. IN ABOUT SIX WEEKS YOUR BULBS SHOULD BLOOM. STAGGER PLANTINGS ABOUT ONE WEEK APART TO ENSURE YOU'LL HAVE BLOOMS FOR A HOLIDAY PARTY OR SPECIAL EVENT.

AMARYLLIS NEED A DORMANT PERIOD AND COOL TEMPERATURES BEFORE THEY BLOOM. WHEN YOU PURCHASE A NEW BULB, IT HAS USUALLY BEEN PRETREATED BY THE GROWER, AND A FLOWER BUD IS ALREADY PUSHING UP. A SECOND FLOWER BUD MAY FOLLOW, WITH FOLIAGE APPEARING AFTER THE BLOOM. RELAX! NO MATTER HOW HARD YOU TRY TO GET THE TIMING RIGHT, THE NATURAL WORLD RUNS ON ITS OWN SCHEDULE. THE NUMBER OF HOURS OF SUNLIGHT, THE TEMPERATURE OF YOUR ROOM, AND THE WAY THE BULB WAS HANDLED BEFORE YOU GOT IT ALL AFFECT THE TIME IT TAKES FOR A BULB TO BLOOM.

5 Cut the stems of the kale on a slant to a length of 4 inches and insert the stems into the front surface of the foam blocks. You now have the major components of the mantel medley in place.

6 Insert three pieces of the holly vertically into each piece of foam. Repeat with the pine. These stems will balance out the weight of the kale in the foam.

7 Place the small clay pots on the mantel wherever there is room. Top each with an ornament. To make one pot a little taller, I inverted another pot and used it for a stand. Tuck in the other two ornaments among the materials where they will be visible, but won't roll off and break.

8 Fill in with pine and santolina, inserting the stems into the foam blocks. Let some of the materials drape down over the mantle by inserting the stems upward into the foam.

Easter/Spring Mantel

SINCE TIME BEGAN, *the coming of spring and the beginning of the planting season have had enormous significance for humankind. This design features pots of annuals to be planted in the yard when any danger of frost is past.*

BACKYARD BITS
About Eggs

The rhea and ostrich eggs used in the "Easter/Spring Mantel" on page 99 came from two backyards in Hegins Valley, Pennsylvania, not far from my home, where the farmers wanted to try to raise something new. Nice-size goose eggs are often available in specialty food markets, or you may find other sources for quail, pheasant, and other birds' eggs in your neck of the woods. If hens aren't scratching in your own backyard, you know where to buy a dozen white or brown eggs. Decorate them or leave them natural.

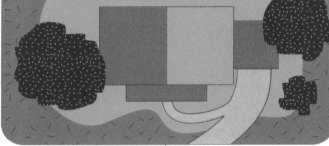

GATHER YOUR MATERIALS

For a 6¼-foot-long mantel

16 stems of fan-tail willow, fresh or dried
20 to 24 stems of weeping willow, 2 to 4 feet long
2 daisy plants
2 pots of geraniums
2 six-pack containers of pansies (Here I used yellow and "antique-shade" pansies.)
Green sheet moss, dampened
4 or 5 watering cans, depending on the size of your mantel (You can use old or new ones.)
Eggs, with the insides blown out (Here I used 2 ostrich eggs, 5 rhea eggs, and 3 other eggs I had on hand. See "Sources" on page 202 for a mail-order source for ostrich eggs.)
2 baskets, for the eggs and daisy plants
Glass vase or other tall container to serve as an egg stand
3 thick rubber bands
Clippers

PUT THEM ALL TOGETHER

1 Place the watering cans along the mantel according to your design. Put the fan-tail willow stems in one can, where desired.

2 Divide the stems of weeping willow into three bunches. Secure each with a rubber band. Place each bunch behind a watering can or other object, hiding the ends and letting the tips drape down over the mantel.

3 Put some of the eggs in one basket and the daisy plants in another and position the baskets on the mantel, along with the two pots of geraniums.

4 Set the packs of pansies along the mantel, or divide them up into individual plants, wrapping each one in dampened sheet moss.

5 Drape more of the sheet moss strategically along the mantel, hiding the plastic pots and packs, tucking pieces here and there, unifying the design. Piles of the moss also can serve as nests for the eggs.

6 Add the remaining eggs wherever they will show the best in your mantel design. Here, one is in the mouth of a watering can and another rests in a tall glass vase.

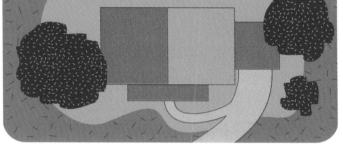

BACKYARD BITS
Mantel Medleys

When it comes to decorating mantels, the look is lavish and exuberant. You pile, stuff, pack, and drape materials to form a theme. The secret is to have on hand a greater quantity of things than you think you'll need: more branches, more filler, more flowers. A variety of materials makes the medley interesting, but repetitions of the same will draw the length of the mantel together. If you have to choose between more of the same and something different, you might be better off with more of the same.

Flower Power

Easy to Care for, Fresh or Dried FAN-TAIL WILLOW, A CONTORTED FORM OF PUSSY WILLOW, DRIES EASILY AND LASTS FOREVER IF LEFT IN A CONTAINER WITHOUT WATER. LIKE PUSSY WILLOW, IT ROOTS IF FRESHLY CUT STEMS STAND IN A VASE OF WATER FOR ABOUT EIGHT WEEKS. WHEN PLANTING OUT IN THE GARDEN, MAKE SURE TO GIVE EACH STEM AT LEAST 10 FEET OF GROWING ROOM AND KEEP THE ROOTS MOIST DURING THE FIRST SEASON.

Christmas Tree

A CHRISTMAS TREE STRUNG WITH FAIRY LIGHTS is a shining showcase of simple decorations from the yard. Paint, ribbon, and ice cream cones are the only other purchased necessities. No one with a fear of heights was allowed to decorate this tree, which was perched on a small landing overlooking a dining room.

GATHER YOUR MATERIALS

For a 9-foot tree (adjust the quantities for the size of your tree)

- 36 ice-cream cone ornaments (See "Silver Cones" on page 105 for instructions.)
- 50 slices of osage orange ornaments (See "Osage-Orange Discs" on page 106 for instructions.)
- 50 large pinecone ornaments (See "Shimmery Pinecones" on page 107 for instructions.)
- 75 hydrangea heads
- 50 half-handfuls of pennycress (You can substitute wild mustard pods or any dried leaf.)
- Mixed dried bouquet tied with a ribbon for the tree topper
- 50 stems of money plant
- 25 silver bows
- 25 gold bows
- 25 white-and-gold bows
- Gold spray paint
- Silver spray paint
- Floral spool wire
- Rubber bands
- Paper clips or ornament hangers
- Clippers

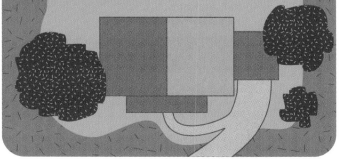

BACKYARD BITS

Trimming the Tree

A large tree seems to devour ornaments. Ensure you'll have enough by using materials you have in abundance. This is a good way to use up your old or faded natural materials that still have structural integrity because you'll be spray painting over them. I chose pennycress over goldenrod, even though I have masses of both, because its flat surface reflects the light more completely and gives the silver paint a higher sheen. Also, my pennycress faded from green to beige by holiday time, so I was happy to see it make a royal exit.

Osage-Orange Discs

Osage Indians of Arkansas and Missouri once used the wood of the osage orange tree for bows and arrows. Settlers planted the thorny trees in hedgerows to fence the prairie. The big green fruit is now used for large fall arrangements and for little boys to throw at each other and smash in the street. Dried slices of osage orange are transformed into ornaments with decorative seed patterns.

GATHER YOUR MATERIALS

Osage oranges (They are also called hedge apples.)
Gold spray paint
Paper clips or ornament hangers
Paring knife

PUT THEM ALL TOGETHER

1 Using the paring knife, cut each osage orange into slices about ½ inch thick. Discard the ends.

2 Dry the slices in an oven or dehydrator. (See "Seven Methods of Preserving Flowers and Herbs" on page 194.)

3 Spray paint both sides gold in a well-ventilated area and set the slices aside to dry.

4 Insert open paper clips or ornament hangers into the oranges and set them aside until you are ready to hang them on the tree.

shimmery Pinecones

The most difficult part of this project is collecting the pinecones; you can get around this by purchasing the cones at your local garden center.

GATHER YOUR MATERIALS

50 large pinecones
Silver spray paint
Paper clips or ornament hangers

PUT THEM ALL TOGETHER

1 Spray paint the pinecones silver in a well-ventilated area and set them aside to dry.

2 Insert open paper clips or ornament hangers into the pinecones and set them aside until you are ready to hang them on the tree.

*T*able Tree à la California

IF YOU HAVE NO ROOM *or desire for a full-fledged fir or spruce, here is a Norfolk Island pine to cherish long after the holidays are gone. Simply remove the decorations and continue to enjoy your graceful houseplant. The fruit and flower decorations all grow in California but are also available throughout the country at florists and markets. Vary the proportions of the trimmings according to your taste and what's available in your area.*

GATHER YOUR MATERIALS

For a 4-foot-tall tree

Norfolk Island pine or other well-
  formed houseplant tree
30 fresh kumquats
26 dried orange slices(See
  "Seven Methods of Preserving
  Flowers and Herbs" on page 194.)
40 dried cayenne peppers
12 small dried artichokes with hooks
  (Be sure to insert the hooks while
  the artichokes are fresh.)
33 clusters of dried white statice
25 small clusters of dried pink
  pepperberries
12 small bows of ½-inch-wide ribbon
Jardiniere
Floral spool wire
Ribbon decoration for the jardiniere
  (optional)
Clippers

NOTE: This tree stands against a wall so the back was left undecorated. If your tree will be seen from all sides, increase the number of decorations by approximately one-fourth.

PUT THEM ALL TOGETHER

1 Put the plant in the jardiniere and set it in its permanent spot. Add a bow if the jardiniere looks too plain.

2 Cut 4- to 6-inch pieces of spool wire to make the ornament hooks. Shape each piece of wire into an S and insert it into a kumquat, orange slice, or cayenne pepper. Hang these plus the artichoke ornaments on the tree.

3 Tie the bows to the tree with the floral spool wire and lay the statice and pepperberries on the branches.

Sweet Texas Tree

FRESH-CUT SUGARCANE, *gleaming like mahogany in the sun, inspired this tree that I designed in the folk-art tradition. I learned that five 4-foot canes are backbreaking to carry through airports from Texas to Pennsylvania, but as the juices dry out they do get lighter. Louisiana is a prime sugarcane state, but I happened to spy these in Texas.*

GATHER YOUR MATERIALS

Five 4-foot lengths of sugar cane (This is available at some specialty produce markets, or you can substitute thick corn stalks or tree branches that are about 1 inch in diameter.)

9 piñon cones (You can substitute pinecones.)

10 clumps of tree beard (You can substitute Spanish moss.)

Celosia (optional)

9 milkweed birds (See "Milkweed Larks" on page 113 for instructions.)

4 cookie birds (See "Cookie Birds" on page 115 for instructions.)

7 glass bird ornaments (See "Backyard Bits—Sprucing Up Purchased Ornaments" on page 114.)

(continued)

Gather Your Materials – *Continued*

Old plastic pot and mixing stick
Jardiniere
Floral spool wire
2-inch finishing nails
Newspapers
Plaster of paris
Water
Ribbon, ¼-inch wide, 12-inch length
    for each ornament
Saw
Hammer
Glue gun and glue sticks

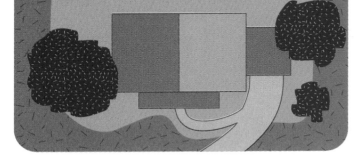

BACKYARD BITS
Cookie Trees

Because the tree shape is a timeless and universal motif, once the "Sweet Texas Tree" on page 110 is constructed it can be decorated for other holidays and special occasions. For Valentine's Day, use heart-shaped cookies; for Easter, suspend decorated eggs and bunny cookies by pastel ribbons; and for a kitchen shower, suspend unusual cookie cutters along with the cookies and add handy utensils like a melon-ball cutter, vegetable peeler, and a lemon zester.

Favorite cookie cutters in my collection are those that were handed down to me by my mother and include the bird used for this tree. My own children seemed to prefer using the red plastic elephant and lion cutters, which I bought as a young mother, to the "antique" cutters I used as a child.

PUT THEM ALL TOGETHER

1 Lay the canes out on the floor and form the basic shape. If the canes are uneven lengths, use the longest for the center post. The other three canes will form the sloping sides and the bottom. With the saw cut the last cane into two pieces to form the other horizontal bars. Here the bars are 16 and 24 inches long.

2 Bind the three pieces at the top with the spool wire. Next, bind the sloping sides to the horizontal bars with the wire. To make the tree sturdier, hammer finishing nails into the places where the canes meet.

3 Use the newspaper to protect your work surface. Follow the package directions and mix the plaster of paris and water in the old pot.

4 Insert the tree trunk into the plaster mixture. You may have to hold the trunk upright until the plaster is firm enough to support it. Allow at least another 24 hours to complete drying before you move the tree to the spot where you will decorate it. When the plaster is fully dry, insert the pot in the jardiniere and begin to decorate.

5 Glue on the piñon cones and the clumps of tree beard. Cover the plaster and pot with the remaining tree beard.

6 Hang the ornaments as desired with the pieces of ribbon. The glass bird ornaments all had clips instead of the typical hangers, so I clipped them to pieces of tree beard. If the clips show, hide them with small tufts of tree beard.

Fanciful Birds

THREE BIRD SPECIES ADORN THE SUGARCANE TREE, *all rarae aves. The purchased glass ornaments sport decorations from the garden, the sugar cookies are an endangered species, and the milkweed larks are the rarest of all because you create them in your workshop.*

Milkweed Larks

These ornaments are a great way to use up leftover paint. Here the "female" is my old bedroom color, and the brighter "male" is my new color.

GATHER YOUR MATERIALS

For one bird

2 halves of a common milkweed pod
1 small nut with a peaked end, like a
    chestnut or filbert
1 big thorn

(continued)

Gather Your Materials — *Continued*

    Cockscomb (optional)
    Floral spool wire or other thin wire,
       4-inch length
    Paint (You can use leftover wall paint
       or spray paint.)
    Clippers
    Glue gun and glue sticks

PUT THEM ALL TOGETHER

1 Cut one-half of the milkweed pod in half again, lengthwise. These will be the wings of the bird.

2 Take the uncut half, which will be the body, and glue on the nut for the head. Glue on the thorn for the beak.

3 Glue the two cut pieces of milkweed pod to the sides of the body to form the bird's wings.

4 Push the ends of the wire through the "shoulders" and tie underneath. You now have a small loop for hanging. As you do this, check the balance of the bird to see that the position of the loop will allow the bird to hang horizontally.

BACKYARD BITS
Sprucing Up Purchased Ornaments

Not every decoration on the "Sweet Texas Tree" was made from scratch. I purchased the seven glass bird ornaments you see in the photo on pages 110–111, but they came with ugly plastic tails and feathers. I carefully removed them and glued small pieces of red cockscomb in their place to make the birds more to my liking. Experiment with different types of dried flowers to see what works with your own ornaments.

5 Paint the bird and let it dry. Use spray paint or dip the bird in a can of leftover wall paint.

6 Glue on the cockscomb, if desired, to represent feathers. Here the "females" have a red breast.

Cookie Birds

These cookie ornaments are edible, but have fewer calories when hanging on a tree.

GATHER YOUR MATERIALS

Ingredients to make your favorite
  sugar cookie recipe
Colored sugar
Nuts or raisins for the eyes and beaks
Cookie cutter in the shape of a bird
Skewer, straw, or toothpick

PUT THEM ALL TOGETHER

1 Make the sugar cookie recipe, but roll out the dough slightly thicker than recommended.

2 Cut out the shapes with the cookie cutter. Sprinkle on colored sugar and press in bits of nuts or raisins for the eyes and beaks.

3 Bake according to the recipe. As soon as you remove the cookies from the oven, poke a hole through the upper back using the skewer, straw, or toothpick. (If you poke the hole before baking, it will fill in as the cookie rises.) Be sure to make the hole large enough for the ribbon to go through.

4 Remove from the cookie sheet to a cooling rack. Store the completely cooled cookies until you're ready to hang them on the tree.

Very Virginia Topiary

Boxwood hedges border *the formal gardens of colonial homes. Regular clipping maintains a meticulous appearance. Since boxwood dries well and keeps its color, put the clippings to good use in holiday arrangements that will outlast the holiday.*

Gather Your Materials

2 bushel baskets of boxwood trimmings, fresh or dried, at least 3 inches long
40 stems of yarrow or other dried flower
Chicken wire, 40 inches high, 1-yard length
Jardiniere
1 sturdy stick, 2 to 3 feet high
2 to 3 bricks of brown floral foam
Floral spool wire
Decorations as desired (Here I used one star at the top and a bow made of 2 yards of wired ribbon.)
Lazy Susan (optional)
Paring knife
Clippers

Put Them All Together

1 Form the shape of the topiary by rolling the chicken wire and pinching in where necessary. Here I chose a modified diamond. You can also form a sphere or several spheres of different sizes. Secure the shape by folding in the ends of the chicken wire.

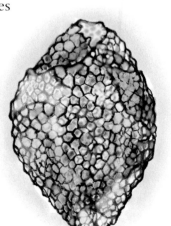

2 Insert the stick into the shape and tie it securely to the chicken wire in several places with the spool wire.

3 Using the paring knife, trim the foam to fit the jardiniere and stuff it in securely, completely covering the opening.

4 Cut the bottom of the stick to a point, and insert the topiary frame into the middle of the foam.

5 The hard work is done; now take your time and stuff the boxwood into the chicken wire. Place the topiary on the lazy Susan, if desired. Start at the top and work downward, turning the frame as you go. If you're using fresh boxwood, remember that the leaves will shrink as they dry, so make the form very full or go back in about a week and add more leaves where needed.

6 Trim the boxwood where it is uneven, shearing the shrub in the same manner you would outside.

7 Cover the floral foam with the yarrow, cutting the stems as short as needed and inserting them into the foam.

8 Remove the topiary from the lazy Susan and decorate it, as desired. I added a star and a bow for the holiday season.

The Kansas Wreath

MY FRIEND DR. CHAD TELLS ME *that martynia, or devil's claw, grows wild in his home state of Kansas and attacks the ankles of grazing cattle and hikers. I sow it in my garden where I can corral the plants into a small plot and harvest the unruly pods. Their whorls and swirls breathe movement into any wreath or arrangement.*

GATHER YOUR MATERIALS

14 clusters of fresh pine and arborvitae, 6 to 8 stems per cluster

5 martynia pods (You can substitute milkweed pods or pinecones.)

13 to 15 dried dahlia heads (Here I used red and yellow ones.)

10 stems of wild rose hips

14-inch wreath frame with 14 clamps

Gold ribbon, 3-yard length (Here I used mesh ribbon that spreads from 3 to 5 inches wide.)

Floral spool wire

Clippers

Glue gun and glue sticks

PUT THEM ALL TOGETHER

1 To make the wreath, clamp the greens cluster by cluster in the wreath frame. Lay the first cluster of greens in a clamp and bend the wires tightly shut.

2 Place the next cluster on top of the stems of the first and clamp. Continue around the frame in this manner.

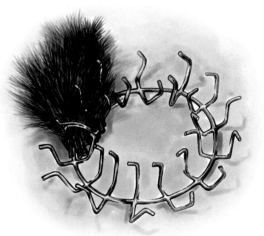

3 Make a bow with long tails using the gold ribbon, and wire it to the wreath. Allow the tails to drape down along the wreath.

4 Glue on the pods, dahlias, and rose hips. If using martynia, face the points inward to avoid impaling unsuspecting family and friends.

Don't Mess with Texas

OFFICIAL-LOOKING SIGNS *along the highways of South Texas proclaim "Don't Mess with Texas." I don't know if they are an antilittering campaign or an injunction to the competitors of the Cowboys. Thorny plant material makes an airy and textured base for wreaths and swags. Mess with it at your peril, and always treat it with respect.*

GATHER YOUR MATERIALS

4 to 6 stems of a "white brush," a mixture of thorny, leafless branches like hardy orange and mesquite

4 stems of fresh firethorn

2 balls of tree beard (You can substitute Spanish moss.)

Ribbon, 1½ to 2 inches wide, 1½-yard length

3 cutout stars, made of silver oak tag or plain oak tag sprayed silver

Handful of silver angel hair (This can be purchased at a Christmas shop.)

Floral spool wire

Clippers

Glue gun and glue sticks

PUT THEM ALL TOGETHER

1 To make the frame of white brush, divide the stems into two equal piles. Place the piles end to end with an overlap of several inches. Bind tightly in the middle with spool wire.

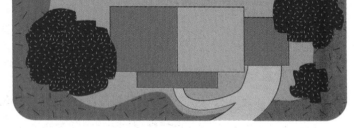

BACKYARD BITS
Firethorn

The materials used in "Don't Mess with Texas" on the opposite page were sent to me in mid-November by Ed Ware of San Antonio, and they were still in good condition when this photo was taken in early January. As always, the climate and the location of the swag will determine how long the firethorn and other materials will last, though the cooler the temperature the better. When firethorn is completely dried, it tends to drop berries, so I don't recommend hanging it on a door that gets used regularly.

2 Divide the firethorn into two equal piles and bind one to each side of the white brush swag.

3 Make a simple bow with the ribbon, and tie that to the middle of the swag with a piece of wire.

4 Impale the balls of tree beard with the swag. The thorns will hold them in place.

5 Cut out the three silver stars. Bend the points inward if you want to make them three dimensional. Glue them to the swag.

6 Angel hair comes in a very tight clump. Gently stretch it out until it resembles a cobweb and drape it over the swag.

*P*rincesses and Angels

PRINCESS PINE, *or <u>Lycopodium</u>, gathered in the fall in Wisconsin, sports lovely "candles" sprouting from the tops of its shoots. The greens are long-lasting when cut, and they dry without shattering. This pine may be protected in some areas so check before you pick, or purchase it from a reputable garden center when the Christmas greens come in. These greens are especially lovely combined with hand-crafted angels.*

GATHER YOUR MATERIALS

2- to 3-gallon bucketful of cut princess pine
Large acorn, one per angel
Medium-size pinecone, one per angel
Whole milkweed pod, one per angel
2 stems of purple statice per angel
20 small globe amaranth flowers per angel
Oriental nigella pod, one per angel (You can substitute a translucent pod from a money plant.)

(continued)

Gather Your Materials — *Continued*

Green sheet moss, about 16 inches square (It can be pieced together.)

14-inch straw wreath base

25 to 35 floral pins

Three 4-inch candles, for decoration only (optional)

Floral spool wire or other thin wire, 10-inch length

Ribbon, 2 to 3 inches wide, 3-yard length

Clippers

Glue gun and glue sticks

BACKYARD BITS
Cones and Pods

Large conifer cones are interchangeable in this project. You can substitute cones from different species to produce angels of a different size and shape.

Lotus pods (available from most dried flower centers) are useful to create short bell-shaped angels with "gathered" skirts.

PUT THEM ALL TOGETHER

1 Moisten the sheet moss and press out the excess water. Drape it over the top and sides of the wreath form.

2 Take 4 or 5 stems of princess pine and attach them to the wreath base with a floral pin. Take another 4 or 5 stems and pin on an angle on the outside edge of the base. You will ultimately fill in and cover the entire wreath by pinning small clusters of pine over the stems of the previous clusters.

3 To make the angel, glue the acorn to the top of the cone. You may have to cut off the stem and tip of the cone to make a seat for the acorn.

4 Split the milkweed pod in half. Carefully remove the inner membrane that runs along the inside of the pods. Glue the pod halves to the back of the cone, sticking up to form the angel's wings, as shown in the photo on page 122. Glue the two pieces of membrane to the sides of the cone to make the arms.

5 Wrap the 10-inch piece of wire around the "waist" of the angel and twist tightly.

6 Glue small pieces of statice to the insides of the wings for color. Glue the globe amaranth flowers between the "petals" of the cone, with the smaller flowers near the head and the larger ones toward the base.

7 Glue on the halo. Here I slit open a pod of oriental nigella, or you could use the oval pod of the money plant.

8 Make as many angels as you desire. Here I used three for a 14-inch wreath. Attach the angels by wrapping the wire around the wreath.

9 Tuck the ribbon in puffs around the wreath. Attach it at a few places with a floral pin.

10 If using candles, attach each with a floral pin to the straw base. As the wreath dries, it will become highly flammable, so **do not light the candles**—use them for decoration only.

11 To prolong the life of the princess pine, keep the wreath outdoors or in a cool spot and mist it occasionally with water.

Collage
Compositions

Corn leaves
resemble a
tropical species
when picked
green and
air-dried.

Paste together bits and pieces of natural materials and transform them into something else entirely. Keep the project totally natural or add other scraps from your collection: special papers, buttons, ribbon, or lace. Your design will evolve from a simple beginning into a unique composition of materials.

Dry the fan-shaped leaves of the South Carolina palmetto tree and craft a fireplace screen.

Take a walk through the woods of Colorado to hunt for fallen birch, aspen, and other barks to use in natural crafts.

The Roses Are Everywhere Collage

I USED NINE SILICA-DRIED ROSE BLOSSOMS *in an old frame that was missing its glass to create a floral collage. The yellow roses are 'Golden Showers', the smaller pink ones are 'Royal Bonica', the single large rose is 'Cary Grant', the whitish one is 'Garden Party', and the gold and orange rose is 'Rio Samba'.*

GATHER YOUR MATERIALS

9 rose blossoms dried in silica gel (See "Seven Methods of Preserving Flowers and Herbs" on page 194.)
Handful of rose petals
35 air-dried rosebuds
Pink, acid-free mat board
Frame (Here I used one with an interior size of 9 by 14 inches.)
Old lace
Antique postcard
Calling card
6 pieces of Victorian-style paper
White craft glue
X-Acto knife
Sealing spray

PUT THEM ALL TOGETHER

1 Using the X-Acto knife, carefully cut the mat board to fit the frame and glue it in place.

2 Spray the roses, front and back, with several coats of sealing spray. Set them aside to dry.

3 Plan your display. Glue the larger objects first, then the smaller items, allowing some to overlap. Here the lace and postcard form the bottom layer.

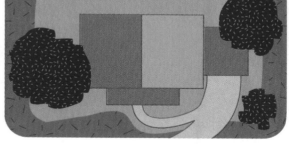

BACKYARD BITS
Frame First

Start your collage with a frame, antique or ready-made. The frame most often will dictate the design. Most items will be three-dimensional, so use either a shadowbox frame with glass or a flat frame without the glass. Keep your first collage fairly small, no larger than 12 by 14 inches, so you won't be daunted. Have small scissors, craft glue, and a glue gun and glue sticks handy.

The New Jersey Shore Collage

MY PERSISTENT IMAGE OF THE
*New Jersey shore features bright
blue hydrangeas and brilliant
geraniums flourishing throughout
the summer in the sandy gardens
in front of the beach houses. I've
captured that scene in a collage of
natural materials. Add mementos
from vacations and holidays to
create a personal collage.*

GATHER YOUR MATERIALS

Seashells
Tree bark
Dried marsh grass and leaves
Dried hydrangea head, divided into
    several pieces
Waxed geraniums (See "Flower
    Power—Wax in Batches" on
    page 18 and "Seven Methods of
    Preserving Flowers and Herbs"
    on page 194.)
Pretty papers (Here I used navy and
    mottled blue and white paper.)
Frame with mat or paper background
    (Here I used one with an interior
    size of 8 by 10 inches.)
White craft glue
Scissors
Glue gun and glue sticks

PUT THEM ALL TOGETHER

1 Glue one sheet of paper to the back
of the frame with the craft glue. Wet
and crumple the other paper for the cloud
and glue it in place where desired. Here
I used the mottled paper for the background and the navy paper for the cloud.

2 Glue on the other materials in a
pleasing pattern. It helps to lay the
elements out on your worktable to determine the arrangement before you glue
them in place. Again, I've allowed some
of the leaves and flowers to escape the
confines of the frame.

130

Flower Power

Geraniums OF THE 10,000 OR MORE SPECIES AND CULTIVARS OF GERANIUMS
THAT HAVE BEEN IDENTIFIED, SCENTED GERANIUMS HAVE BECOME FAVORITES OF HERB
GROWERS. THEY'RE GROWN FOR THEIR AROMA RATHER THAN FOR THEIR INSIGNIFICANT
FLOWERS, ON THE WINDOWSILL OR IN THE GARDEN, BRUSH BY A LEAF TO RELEASE THE
GLORIOUS AROMA. 'ATTAR OF ROSES' IS A FAVORITE OF MINE. I PLANT SOME TO SNIFF
AS I WEED THE GARDEN AND USE THE DRIED LEAVES IN MANY POTPOURRI RECIPES.

The New Hampshire Collage

IT'S MID-MAY IN NEW HAMPSHIRE, and in the bottom of my daughter's garden the ferns are just springing forth. (Several varieties were planted years ago.) Some are in full leaf, some in bud, and some sturdy pods have wintered over from last summer's growth. I beg her for a contribution, which she willingly grants me.

GATHER YOUR MATERIALS

9 or 10 pieces of pressed fern leaf, 3 to 6 inches long (See "Seven Methods of Preserving Flowers and Herbs" on page 194.)

22 fern stems dried in the bud stage (See "Backyard Bits—Drying Fern Buds," at right)

6 stems of sensitive fern pod

Frame with mat or paper background (Here I used one with an interior size of 10 inches square.)

Bow of satin cording or ribbon

White craft glue

Ruler

Pencil

Scissors

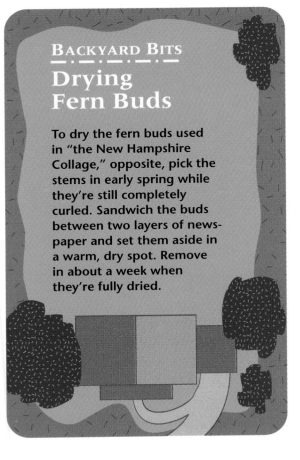

BACKYARD BITS
Drying Fern Buds

To dry the fern buds used in "the New Hampshire Collage," opposite, pick the stems in early spring while they're still completely curled. Sandwich the buds between two layers of newspaper and set them aside in a warm, dry spot. Remove in about a week when they're fully dried.

PUT THEM ALL TOGETHER

1 This collage is balanced, but not identical, on both sides. With the ruler find the top and bottom center of the frame and make small marks with the pencil.

2 Glue down eight pieces of pressed fern, fanning them out from the bottom center.

3 Glue a tall piece of fern bud in the center, then fan out the other buds on each side and glue them in place. Cut the stems as necessary. Here the tallest stem is 9¼ inches and the shortest is 2½ inches.

4 Fill in with the sensitive fern pods, cutting the stems as necessary. Use the remaining pressed fern leaves to fill in the bare spots.

5 Glue the bow to the bottom center of the arrangement or wherever you desire.

The Hawaiian Collage

DRIED BOUGAINVILLEA *adds splashes of bright color to dried leaves, bark, and pods gathered from the beach, forest, or garden. Design an abstract collage following your fancy. Perch an orchid nearby to complete the tropical feel.*

GATHER YOUR MATERIALS

Dried banana leaves
Palm bark
Pods
Driftwood
Dried seaweed
Dried bougainvillea "flowers" (See "Flower Power—Ironing Flowers and Leaves" on page 136.)
Frame with mat or paper background (Here I used one with an interior size of 12 by 15 inches.)
White craft glue
Scissors
Glue gun and glue sticks

BACKYARD BITS
Collage Is a State of Mind

Wherever you live, wherever you travel, pay attention to the minutiae of natural life that enhance your experiences. Satisfy your magpie instincts and collect some of the wonderful treasures that you see. Gather a pile of stuff, more than you think you will need, so you can pick and choose as the spirit moves you. Add other bits and pieces like ribbon, lace, scrap, and paper that fit or contrast with the mood of your natural materials. Let the children help you collect, or suggest they make their own collage. This project is a natural for the free-spirited imagination of a young mind. Put on your favorite music and start to play with your stuff. Make the collage fanciful or realistic; let your mind wander away from any second guessing and thoughts of "I can't." Obviously, there is no right or wrong to making a collage, and yours will look totally different from mine because it's based on the materials you've collected as well as your feelings and thoughts at the time you made it. Have fun!

PUT THEM ALL TOGETHER

1 Cover the back of the frame with the dried leaves and bark, cutting the materials as necessary to fit the frame. The pieces overlap and where they didn't lie flat, I allowed them to fan out, making pockets to insert other materials.

2 Experiment with the placement of the other materials, and when satisfied, glue them in place. Although the frame is extremely important in uniting the composition, allow some materials to sneak out over the edge of the frame for movement.

Flower Power
Ironing Flowers and Leaves

IF YOU HAVE JUST A FEW FLOWERS OR LEAVES TO DRY AND NO FLOWER PRESS HANDY, TRY IRONING THEM. HERE I PRESSED THE BOUGAINVILLEA "FLOWERS" BETWEEN TWO LAYERS OF NEWSPAPER WITH MY IRON. PICK THE FLOWERS OR LEAVES OFF THE STEM AND PLACE THEM IN A SINGLE LAYER ON ABSORBENT PAPER. COVER THEM WITH ANOTHER LAYER OF PAPER. SET YOUR IRON ON A MEDIUM-LOW SETTING AND PRESS FOR ABOUT TEN MINUTES, CONSTANTLY MOVING THE IRON, THEN TURN THE WHOLE PACK OVER AND PRESS THE BOTTOM SIDE. THIS TECHNIQUE WORKS WITH FLOWERS THAT ARE RELATIVELY FLAT, BUT NOT FLOWERS LIKE WHOLE ROSES OR CARNATIONS.

Mélange of Papier-Mâché

SELECT A BOTTLE WITH A CLASSIC SHAPE *and add some interesting
pods or grasses. Transform them with papier-mâché into an
unusual accent piece or a vase for dried flowers.*

137

South Carolina Bottle

For the fuchsia bottle I used small seed-pods from the brilliant crape myrtle tree and one southern magnolia pod, all found while I was strolling along the delightful streets of Charleston.

GATHER YOUR MATERIALS

6 clusters of crape myrtle seedpods
1 southern magnolia pod
Materials listed in the "Mélange of Papier-Mâché Project Basics" on page 140
Orange ribbon, ¼ inch wide, cut into strips
Glue gun and glue sticks

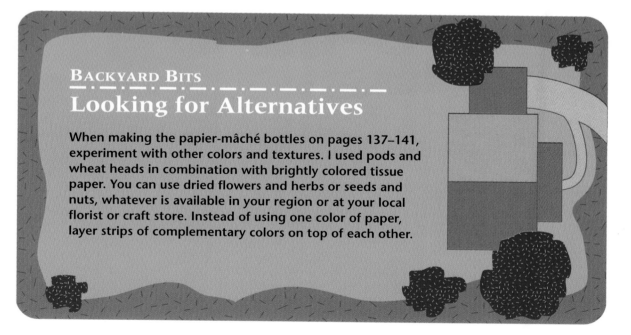

BACKYARD BITS
Looking for Alternatives

When making the papier-mâché bottles on pages 137–141, experiment with other colors and textures. I used pods and wheat heads in combination with brightly colored tissue paper. You can use dried flowers and herbs or seeds and nuts, whatever is available in your region or at your local florist or craft store. Instead of using one color of paper, layer strips of complementary colors on top of each other.

PUT THEM ALL TOGETHER

1 Follow the general instructions in the "Mélange of Papier-Mâché Project Basics" on page 140.

2 Glue on the pods in a pleasing manner. Here I arranged the two types of pods in a random pattern.

3 Paste the strips of orange ribbon over the stems and the neck of the bottle in a pattern of your choosing.

Arizona Bottle

On the gold bottle I used pods found by a friend at a truck stop in Arizona. The owner identified them as "fig," but whatever they are, they're lovely.

GATHER YOUR MATERIALS

6 pods (Use whatever you have available in your area.)
Orange ribbon, ¼ inch wide, cut into strips
Glue gun and glue sticks
Materials listed in the "Mélange of Papier-Mâché Project Basics" on page 140

PUT THEM ALL TOGETHER

1 Follow the general instructions in the "Mélange of Papier-Mâché Project Basics" on page 140.

2 Glue on the pods in a random pattern. Here I glued the six pods to the front of the bottle.

3 Wrap the orange ribbon around the bottle, connecting each of the pods, and glue in place.

MÉLANGE OF PAPIER-MÂCHÉ PROJECT BASICS

FOR EACH ARRANGEMENT

★ Clean bottle

★ 6 sheets of old newspaper

★ 3 or 4 sheets of white paper

★ 1 or 2 sheets of colored tissue

★ Wallpaper paste

★ Small paintbrush, the size of one from a child's watercolor set

★ Lazy Susan (optional)

HOW TO BEGIN

1. Cover the work surface with a few sheets of the newspaper. Mix the wallpaper paste according to the package instructions.

2. Place the bottle on the lazy Susan, if desired, to make it easier to turn the project as you work.

3. Tear newspaper into strips no longer than 6 inches. One by one, dip the strips into the paste. With your fingers, smooth off all excess paste and place the strip on the bottle. The object is to totally cover the bottle with overlapping strips of paper.

4. Cover the bottle with two more layers of newspaper, overlapping in different directions to keep the project smooth and even. Cover the rim of the bottle and down inside the neck at least ½ inch. If, despite your best efforts, the bottle is getting too sloppy with paste, stick on some dry strips of paper; they will immediately absorb the excess and become part of your covering layer.

5. Following the same procedure in Steps 3 and 4, add torn strips of white paper to cover the newsprint.

6. Tear the colored tissue into strips. Without dipping into paste, put a layer on top of the white paper, overlapping and covering the bottle. Where the tissue overlaps, it will look more opaque when it dries; other areas will look more translucent, giving a wonderful stained-glass effect.

7. Let the bottle dry completely; it will take 2 to 3 days. While it is drying, cover the bowl of wallpaper paste and refrigerate to save it for another project.

8. Proceed following the instructions listed in the project directions on pages 137–141.

Arkansas Bottle

Black-bearded wheat heads from Arkansas grace this small salmon bottle. I tucked a few stems of wheat into the bottle to play up the theme.

GATHER YOUR MATERIALS

5 heads of black-bearded wheat
3 or 4 stems of wheat (optional)
Materials listed in the "Mélange of Papier-Mâché Project Basics" on the opposite page
Glue gun and glue sticks

PUT THEM ALL TOGETHER

1 Follow the general instructions in the "Mélange of Papier-Mâché Project Basics" on the opposite page.

2 Glue the heads of black-bearded wheat to the bottle in a random pattern you find pleasing.

3 To make it look like the wheat heads are embedded in the papier-mâché, add more colored tissue. Brush some paste on the bottle with the paintbrush wherever you would like more tissue, then add more strips.

4 Place a few stems of wheat in the bottle, if desired. If you don't have wheat, you can substitute any dried flower or herb.

State(ly) Hatboxes

THE SEASHORE OF THE GEORGIA *coastal islands, an herb garden in Utah, and the woods of West Virginia provided materials to decorate these stately hatboxes.*

The Georgia Hatbox

Peach-colored ribbon represents the famous Georgia fruit and the cotton bolls are from another famous crop. Harvest the sea oats from a perennial garden instead of stripping the dunes of their protective plants.

GATHER YOUR MATERIALS

  6 cotton bolls
12 shells
  8 stems of sea oats
  Peach-colored ribbon, 2½ to 3 inches
     wide, 40-inch length
  Purchased hatbox of any size (Here
     I used a mesh one that was 8 inches
     high by 12 inches in diameter.)
  Clippers
  Scissors
  Tape measure or ruler
  Glue gun and glue sticks

CLOCKWISE FROM LEFT: UTAH HATBOX, GEORGIA HATBOX, WEST VIRGINIA HATBOX

Flower Power

The Cotton Boll COTTON IS GEN-
ERALLY AN ANNUAL PLANT WITH ONE HAR-
VEST PER GROWING SEASON; HOWEVER, IN
FROST-FREE AREAS IT CAN DEVELOP INTO
A SMALL PERENNIAL SHRUB. THE FLOWERS
OF THE COTTON PLANT RESEMBLE THOSE
OF THE HOLLYHOCK, TO WHICH IT IS RE-
LATED. THE FRUIT OF THE COTTON PLANT
IS ACTUALLY THE BOLL. WHILE IT'S BEST
TO CRAFT WITH FULL-SIZE BOLLS THAT
HAVE SPLIT OPEN, YOU CAN PERFORM
"SURGERY" ON IMMATURE BOLLS. SLIT
THE BOLLS OPEN ALONG THEIR RIDGES
AND BAKE THEM ON A CAKE RACK IN A
150°F OVEN FOR ABOUT 3 HOURS. IF
THE COTTON HASN'T BURST OUT FROM
THE BOLL, USE A FORK TO PROD IT ALONG.

PUT THEM ALL TOGETHER

1 To determine the amount of ribbon
to use, measure the lid of the hatbox.
Cut enough peach-colored ribbon to run
across the top of the box and down each
side with an extra inch on each end to
tuck inside. Glue the ribbon in place. Cut
and glue an identical strip at right angles
to the first.

2 Make a traditional bow with the
peach-colored ribbon and glue it
in the center of the lid.

3 Glue on the large shells first and then
the smaller ones. Next, glue on the
cotton bolls and stems of sea oats to
finish the hatbox.

The Utah Hatbox

An herb garden in miniature represents Utah, the beehive state. Sage, chive flowers, poppy pods, top onion, purple basil, marigolds, plus a few pieces of delphinium for the intense blue of the Utah sky, surround a bee skep. Use a mixture of whatever dried flowers and herbs is available in your area.

GATHER YOUR MATERIALS

Dried pieces of herbs, pods, and flowers
(Here I used sage, chive flowers,
poppy pods, top onion, purple basil,
marigolds, and delphinium.)
Purchased bee skep
Purchased hatbox of any size
(Here I used one that was 5½ inches
high by 10 inches in diameter.)
Clippers
Scissors
Tape measure or ruler
Glue gun and glue sticks

PUT THEM ALL TOGETHER

1 Glue the bee skep in place in the center of the lid of the box. Wait for the glue to dry before going on to the next step so the bee skep won't shift.

2 Glue the dried materials around the skep, beginning with the larger pieces and filling in with the smaller items.

The West Virginia Hatbox

This small box uses only a few materials from West Virginia: dark blue-green ribbon for the woods and forests, four copper-colored leaves from the state flower—the rhododendron—and four half-shells of chestnut pods given to me by my friend Bob Morrison from his mother's yard.

GATHER YOUR MATERIALS

4 pressed rhododendron leaves (See "Seven Methods of Preserving Flowers and Herbs" on page 194.)
4 halves of a chestnut pod
Purchased hatbox of any size (Here I used one that was 4 inches high by 8 inches wide.)
Dark blue-green ribbon, 1½ to 2 inches wide, 40-inch length
Copper spray paint
Clippers
Scissors
Tape measure or ruler
Glue gun and glue sticks

PUT THEM ALL TOGETHER

1 To determine the amount of ribbon to use, start by measuring the bottom of the hatbox. Cut enough ribbon to run one length from 1 inch inside the box, down the side, across the bottom and up the other side, leaving an extra inch to tuck inside the box. Glue the ribbon in place. Cut and glue an identical strip at right angles to the first.

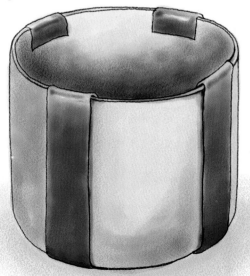

Hatboxes Unlimited

I designed my hatboxes to feature natural materials from three states. Don't limit your hatbox projects to the states and materials I chose to include in this book. Design a hatbox based on where you live, or if you're making a gift, where the recipient lives. Just be aware of any state or federal laws that protect certain plant species and do not gather these plants from the wild. Buy stock or seeds from a reputable nursery. You can substitute any size or shape box with a lid that you have around. Again, my designs are just suggestions; use whatever materials are available to you in your region.

Another set of possibilities opens up when you cover a plain hatbox with papier mâché, following the procedures detailed in "Mélange of Papier-Mâché Project Basics" on page 140. Gather buttons, strands of beads and other fancy findings to decorate the top of the box, either with or without additional dried materials. Those of you who work with silk flowers (and you know who you are) will find opportunities to highlight blossoms from your collection.

2 Measure the lid next, adding an extra inch on each end to tuck inside. Cut two pieces of ribbon to this length.

3 Line up the top with the bottom and glue the ribbons in place so they match and look like a continuation of the bottom ribbons.

4 Make a bow with the dark blue-green ribbon and glue it in place in the center of the lid where the other ribbons intersect.

5 Spray paint the rhododendron leaves copper in a well-ventilated area and set aside to dry.

6 Glue the rhododendron leaves and chestnut pods directly to the top of the hatbox, surrounding the bow.

Nature Tower

IF YOU'RE A HUNTER AND A SAVER, *you already have a complete supply of materials for this project. If you don't have enough natural scrap, share your plans with the children around you; they'll be happy to contribute their treasures. Most of these items come from my own backyard in Pennsylvania; others, like the pheasant feathers, were gifts from friends who know of my peculiar tastes and needs. Thank you to Stephen and Mike Gaffney for the use of the butterfly.*

GATHER YOUR MATERIALS

3 hornets' nests (See "Backyard Bits—Hunting for Materials" on page 150.)

16 dried sunflower heads with or without seeds

10 pieces of birch bark

4 birds' nests

24 dried orange mushrooms

4 assorted clumps of bracken

3 birds' eggshells

Butterfly, cicada shells or other found treasures

6 dried teasels

3 wasps' nests (See "Backyard Bits—Hunting for Materials" on page 150.)

15 twigs and branches

9 pheasant feathers (You can substitute any other kind of feather.)

12 dried oak leaves

12 dried corn leaves

2 dried gourds

8 locust tree pods

12 catalpa tree pods

3 Kentucky coffee tree pods

3 bundles of stems (trimmed from the bottom of any grain) secured with a rubber band

1 bushel basket of moss

Tepee tomato cage

Chicken wire, 40 inches high, 3-yard length

Wire cutter

Clippers

Floral spool wire

Glue gun and glue sticks

Hand drill with small bit (optional)

Hunting for Materials

To make the "Nature Tower" on page 148, use what you can gather in your area and fill in with purchased materials when necessary. Driftwood, shells, grasses, stones, and bark of all kinds are just a few suggestions. Are you game for bones, molted snake skins, and dried-out turtle shells? Collect birds' nests that have fallen after heavy storms and hornets' nests ,in winter when they're empty. Check with your county extension agent if you're in doubt about what and when to collect.

Take extra care when you are gathering hornets' and wasps' nests. First, watch the nest carefully to make sure it's abandoned. Then, to kill any larvae that may still be in the nest, place the nest in a large plastic bag in a freezer that is 0°F or colder for two weeks. It's best to store hornets' nests and other gathered material for this project outdoors in a protected area until you're ready to use them.

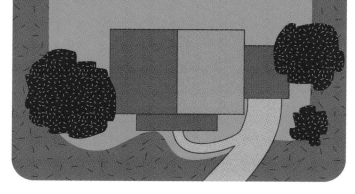

PUT THEM ALL TOGETHER

1 To make the base of the tower, turn the tomato cage so that the wide part is at the bottom. Wrap the chicken wire twice around the cage. Squeeze the top of the wire to make it conform to the conical shape of the tomato cage. Secure it by tucking in the ends of the chicken wire around the cage.

2 Attach the materials in one of three ways. Wire large items, like the hornets' nests, big pieces of bark, and sunflowers, to the form with small lengths of spool wire. Glue on small items like the mushrooms. When the construction gets full, stick other items like the moss and pods with stems into the form.

Indoor/Outdoor Options

The "Nature Tower" on page 148 is designed to be displayed in a protected setting outdoors; however, with a few substitutions it can be made suitable for indoors. Replace the hornets' and wasps' nests, birds' nests, mushrooms, and eggshells with additional dried flowers, pods, twigs, and barks. Use Spanish moss instead of the bracken. Or add purchased materials, if you desire. Remember, it's supposed to be a hodge-podge of assorted elements. If you think you won't have enough materials to cover the chicken wire, start with a smaller tomato cage. There is no right or wrong way to do this project.

3 Start with the largest, heaviest looking items and attach them to the form with 6 to 8 inches of spool wire. To keep the roughly conical shape, place the largest objects toward the bottom of the form. Spread them out at your workspace and distribute them randomly. Wrap the wire through or around the object and attach it to the frame. You may have to poke a hole in some items like the sunflower heads. Use a twig or a small drill for this purpose.

4 Keep adding objects, working upward and turning the form as you go. Add the smaller items, leaving spaces to be filled in later.

5 When the major items have been attached, fill in the whole tower with moss. Simply poke moss partway through the chicken wire to hold it on the surface. The more large items you have, the less moss you'll need, and vice versa.

6 Poke twigs and feathers through the moss. Secure with wire, if necessary, but most will hold as is.

7 Glue the smaller items like the birds' eggshells and mushrooms directly to the moss or bark.

8 Finish by adding a butterfly, cicada shells, or other natural treasures. Display this design in a protected, outdoor spot. Here we photographed the "Nature Tower" on a front porch with an overhead roof.

*T*hree Frame-Ups

MAKE YOUR OWN FRAMES *to personalize photos, mirrors, invitations, and important certificates. Each frame features natural materials from a different state or region and gives you ideas on how to use the materials available in your area.*

152

Southern Live Oak Frame

For people who live throughout much of the South and Southeast, live oaks provide graceful shade. These long-lived trees often grow as wide as they do high, reaching from 30 to 50 feet.

Use the branches in arrangements and wreaths and the tough, leathery leaves for air drying and craft work. Use the elongated acorns to add color and shape to your project.

BACKYARD BITS
Make Your Own Frame

Make an inexpensive frame in no time at all by buying wooden canvas stretchers in a craft or art supply shop. The sides are sold separately and are available in many lengths, from 6 to over 30 inches. Customize your frame size and shape; buy four pieces the same length for a square frame or two pairs of two lengths for a rectangular frame. They need no gluing to assemble; the tongue-and-groove edges slide together easily. Stretcher frames work best when no glass is required for your project and the rough finish is completely covered with flowers or decoupage.

GATHER YOUR MATERIALS

Dried live oak leaves
Bits of twig (optional)
Live oak acorns
Old or cheap purchased frame (Here I used a 9- by 12-inch frame.)
Clippers
Cool-melt glue gun and glue sticks (Hot glue may discolor the leaves.)

PUT THEM ALL TOGETHER

1 Glue the dried leaves onto the frame using the cool-melt glue and glue gun, overlapping the leaves as you go. When the frame is covered, glue a leaf on diagonally at each corner and add a bit of twig, if desired.

2 Glue acorns to the leaves at the top, bottom and sides, as shown at left, or in the four corners or any way you prefer. Add a few extra leaves to the acorn clusters.

NOTE: Bake acorns and other wild nuts at 250°F for two to three hours to avoid emerging pests. Glue the caps back onto the nuts if they loosen while drying.

Jumping Cholla from Arizona

Don't touch fresh cholla when it is covered with sharp and dangerous spines. Instead, look for canes (branches) that have dropped off this miniature tree in the cactus family. Over time the flesh and spines disintegrate and leave these slotted wood canes.

GATHER YOUR MATERIALS

6 pieces of weathered jumping cholla canes (Here I used canes that were 12 to 14 inches long.)
Dried wild grasses
Buttons
20-gauge copper wire
Glue gun and glue sticks
Wire cutters

PUT THEM ALL TOGETHER

1 Lay out the pieces of cane as shown below. Begin with the two canes that will make up the vertical sides of the frame. Place two canes for the horizontal sides on top of these, then two more vertical canes. When satisfied with the arrangement, glue each joint in place.

2 Cut off 6 to 8 inches of copper wire and insert it through the slits at the top of the frame to make the hanger.

3 Decorate the frame as desired. Here I found some buttons in my button box that reminded me of the hot Arizona sun. I didn't have enough of one kind to make a repetitive design, so I twisted 12- to 18-inch lengths of copper wire into little discs and added them to the frame.

4 The cholla canes are hollow when dry, so glue in some short grasses or other dried plant material as desired. Here I glued them into the tops and bottoms of the two vertical canes.

Millefleurs from All States

Use an abundance of flowers and pods to cloak a wood frame with soft pastels, vibrant golds, and dark contrasts. The lush mosaic effect prompted me to call this millefleurs, even though I did not use "one thousand flowers."

GATHER YOUR MATERIALS

75 dried strawflower heads, in mixed sizes and colors
13 dried dahlias
12 dried button mums
29 dried love-in-a-mist pods
Old or cheap purchased frame (Here I used a 12- by 14-inch frame, with a 3-inch border.)
Glue gun and glue sticks

PUT THEM ALL TOGETHER

1 Glue all the flowers on the frame in a random fashion, taking care to cover it completely.

2 To keep the flowers evenly spaced, work from each of the corners and down the sides a little bit at a time until the frame is covered.

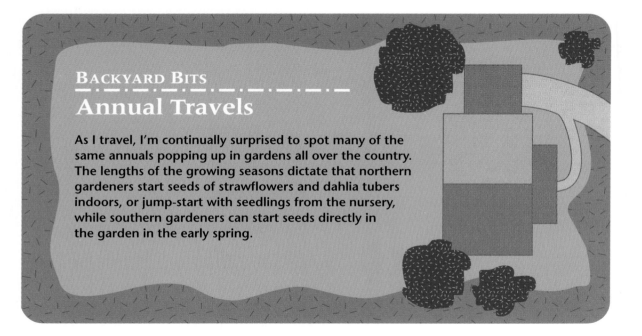

BACKYARD BITS
Annual Travels

As I travel, I'm continually surprised to spot many of the same annuals popping up in gardens all over the country. The lengths of the growing seasons dictate that northern gardeners start seeds of strawflowers and dahlia tubers indoors, or jump-start with seedlings from the nursery, while southern gardeners can start seeds directly in the garden in the early spring.

Birch-Bark Birdhouse

TRAMP THROUGH THE WOODS *in New England in any season to admire the paper-birch trees. The bark peels and sheds easily, and the limbs are somewhat weak. After a storm whole branches are downed and ready to be stripped of their bark with your handy pocketknife. Form a stylish birdhouse; perhaps a family will set up housekeeping.*

Green Foxtail

Green foxtail grows by the roadsides, in cracks of pavement, in abandoned lots, and between the rows of cornfields. Although foxtail is largely ignored as a weed in the wild, visitors to my barn are often intrigued by the bunches hanging to dry. If picked in early August when the grain has developed but the seed is not yet ripe, foxtail stays green for several years and is always soft to the touch.

GATHER YOUR MATERIALS

For a birdhouse 11 inches tall by 8½ inches wide at the base

- 10 to 12 strips of pliable bark, like white birch or a mixture of barks (Some should be at least 11 inches high by 3 inches wide. If the pieces are dried out, soak them in water for 12 hours.)
- 30 stems of green foxtail or other grass, both seed stems and leaves
- 4 milkweed pods (You can substitute any other pod or conifer cone.)
- 8-inch straw wreath base
- Piece of twig
- 8-inch round container of thin plastic with a rim (Use the kind that is used to line the baskets of flower arrangements.)
- Staple gun and staples
- Glue gun and glue sticks
- Clippers
- Sturdy rubber band
- Floral spool wire or a hammer and nails

PUT THEM ALL TOGETHER

1 Slip the plastic container into the straw wreath base, as shown below, and staple the rim of the container to the wreath base. The plastic container forms the bottom of the birdhouse. Overlapping panels of birch form the sides.

2 Staple a strip of birch to the wreath base, slanting the top inward. This birdhouse will have a tepee shape with a small opening at the top. Overlap the next piece of bark, and staple it to the wreath base, continuing to slant the top in. Glue the bark strips to each other along the sides. Your bark strips will probably be of irregular sizes and shapes so you'll have to do some cutting and piecing. For some pieces it will be easier to glue than to staple.

3 If you have a piece of bark with a natural knot, use that as the entrance to the house. If not, cut a circle in a bark strip with the clippers before you affix the strip to the house.

4 As always, the last piece is the hardest to attach because you can't get your hand inside. Your best bet is to glue the last strip in place.

5 Bundle the grass seed stems together with the rubber band, trim the bottoms, and insert the bundle into the hole at the top of the tepee. The grasses make an attractive trim and help keep the rain out of the house.

6 Cut one end of the twig into a point and poke it through the bark into the wreath base for a perch. Add glue to make it more secure.

7 Using the glue gun glue on the milkweed pods and foxtail leaves for decoration, where desired.

8 Decide where you want to place the birdhouse. You can nail it to a fence post through the hole in the top, or loop a length of spool wire through the top to hang it from a limb.

BACKYARD BITS
Tree Facts

The paper birch is the most prevalent of the birches and grows in much of the northern United States and Canada. It is referred to as a pioneer tree because it will grow on bare soil and make shade for the next generation of flora, then die. The thin strips of bark were used by the Indians to make canoes, utensils, and roofs for their wigwams. Today the wood is used for spools, toys, clothespins, and birdhouses!

The Little House on the Prairie

WITHOUT A HAMMER, SAW, OR NAILS, *produce a combination bird feeder, birdhouse, and yard sculpture of discarded Lincoln Logs. After the birds peck the seeds from the flower heads, the interesting structure of the house remains.*

GATHER YOUR MATERIALS

17 small dried sunflower heads with seeds

4 ears of strawberry corn and 5 ears of other miniature corn (The pink corn used here is from Shepherd's Garden Seeds. See "Sources" on page 202.)

20 stems of black-bearded wheat

2 stems of dried love-lies-bleeding or other dried flower

Lincoln Logs to build a small house with roof

Foam core

Floral spool wire

Wood glue

Glue gun and glue sticks

Clippers

Ruler

Knife

Pencil

PUT THEM ALL TOGETHER

1 Build a Lincoln Log house with a roof, any size or shape, leaving a small window to entice birds to nest. This one is 14 inches long, including the toolshed at one end, and 9 inches high at the peak.

2 When you are satisfied, disassemble it and glue it back together using wood glue at the joints. If you plan to hang the house, before you glue on the roof, thread 3 feet of spool wire through the small spaces at the ends of the house. Now when the roof is attached, the wire will be ready for hanging.

3 If you plan to use this project as a feeder or sculpture only, omit this step and proceed to Step 4. If this is to be a working birdhouse, it needs a floor. Measure the bottom of the house. Measure the same size onto the foam core and cut out the shape with a knife. Glue the foam core onto the bottom of the house.

4 Glue the sunflowers to the roof to cover. Cut the love-lies-bleeding in pieces and glue the pieces where they will look interesting.

5 Cut off the stems of wheat. Glue them around the bottom of the house and on the roof. Remove the husks from the miniature corn. Glue a few husks to the roof.

6 Glue two ears of strawberry corn to the roof for a chimney. I used the other two at the top of the toolshed.

7 Cut one ear of corn into five thin slices and glue the slices right under the roof line. Glue the other four miniature ears of corn like pillars to the corners of the facade. Trim the ears of corn as necessary to make them fit.

*F*loral Fire Screen

WHEN I TRAVEL THROUGH *the South Carolina lowlands, the palmetto trees lend a distinctly southern air. As I move north along the coast to North Carolina and Virginia, the magnolias and dogwoods confirm that I'm heading home. I used leaves and flowers from all three trees to form this fireplace screen. It covers a yawning black "hole" in my fireplace when it isn't used in spring and summer.*

GATHER YOUR MATERIALS

You can substitute any combination of dried flowers and leaves you have available.

14 dried palmetto leaves (You can purchase these fresh from the florist and air-dry them yourself, or purchase them from a dried flower supplier.)

20 preserved magnolia leaves (You can substitute dried magnolia or rhododendron leaves.)

11 dogwood flowers dried in silica gel (See "Seven Methods of Preserving Flowers and Herbs" on page 194.)

9 peonies dried in silica gel

(continued)

162

BACKYARD BITS
Southern Varieties

Palmettos, or spineless palms, include both trees and shrubs. They are native from Florida to Venezuela and are commonly found in much of the southern United States. The cabbage palmetto is the state tree of South Carolina and Florida and its fleshy leaf bud is used as a vegetable. The Texas palmetto can grow to 50 feet with a trunk that's $2^1/_2$ feet in diameter. The dwarf palmetto appears to be stemless (its trunk is underground), with leaves that are 2 to 3 feet long.

Gather Your Materials—_Continued_

   5 roses dried in silica gel
   Several sheets of newspaper
   Corrugated cardboard from an
      old carton
   Spray paint, any shade of moss
      green
   Pencil
   Scissors
   Glue gun and glue sticks
   X-Acto knife (optional)

PUT THEM ALL TOGETHER

1 To make the form, fold a sheet of newspaper in half. Draw a pattern for the form, adjusting it to the size of your fireplace. Use a fan shape or a modified fan, as I did here, 30 inches wide at the bottom and 21 inches high in the middle. Note that to make both sides equal, you draw only half the shape on the folded paper, cut it out, then open it up for the full pattern. Trim the shape as necessary or rework it until you're satisfied.

2 Place the newspaper pattern on top of the cardboard. Trace the outline of the pattern onto the cardboard, then cut the form out with scissors or an X-Acto knife. Save the leftover cardboard for the following step.

3 Draw two right-angle triangles on another piece of the cardboard, 15 inches high and 7 inches wide at the base and cut them out. With the scissors' point or a knife, lightly score the cardboard triangles 2 inches from the vertical edge. Bend the cardboard along the scored line.

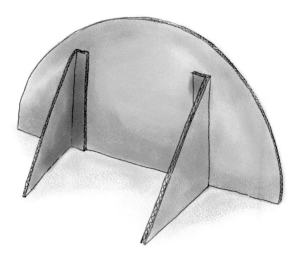

4 Glue the triangles to the back of the fan form equidistant from each edge. Stand the form up to make sure it's level.

5 Spray the front and side edges of the fan form with the green paint, then set aside to dry. Be sure to spray in a well-ventilated area.

6 The floral decoration is all glued to the form with hot glue. Glue down the palmetto leaves first, extending the tops at least 1 inch over the edges of the form to hide it. Fill in the background with magnolia leaves. Next, glue on the peonies, roses, and dogwood.

Flower Power

Screen Legends DOGWOOD IS THE STATE TREE OF MISSOURI AND THE STATE FLOWER AND TREE OF VIRGINIA. IT IS CELEBRATED FOR ITS DELICATE SPRING BLOSSOMS, WHICH ARE ACTUALLY PETAL-LIKE BRACTS. THE TOUGH WOOD IS USED FOR HANDLES FOR TOOLS AND GOLF CLUBS, AS WELL AS FOR WEAVING SHUTTLES.

THE STATE FLOWER OF INDIANA IS THE PEONY, ALTHOUGH MOST VARIETIES ORIGINATED IN ASIA. PEONIES WERE GROWN BY THE RULERS OF CHINA OVER 4,000 YEARS AGO AND WERE AMONG THE FIRST PLANTS TO BE CULTIVATED FOR THEIR FLOWERS.

I DRIED BOTH FLOWERS IN SILICA GEL TO DECORATE THE "FLORAL FIRE SCREEN" ON PAGE 162. I USED TWO DIFFERENT COLORS OF PEONIES HERE, CREAMY WHITE TO MATCH THE DOGWOODS AND DEEP PINK FOR A SHOT OF COLOR. YOU CAN USE ALL ONE COLOR IF YOU PREFER, ADD A THIRD COLOR FOR MORE VARIETY, OR USE DIFFERENT DRIED FLOWERS ALTOGETHER.

Table Decorations

Customarily, a floral centerpiece graces the center of a party table. Embark on a new tradition by using flowers, leaves, shells, and other natural findings to decorate desserts and napkins, or even to replace the tablecloth.

Edible flowers like violas, pansies, and Johnny-jump-ups are perfect for decorating special desserts. Be sure they're organically grown and thoroughly washed.

I planted hollyhocks by my barn before I had even moved to the farm. These "Peach Ruffles" inspired the doll decorations on page 174.

Georgia in January

THE GEORGIA COAST *(Zone 8) in January looks verdant to my snow-jaded northern eyes. While gardeners apologize for their winter shortcomings and try to convince me of the lushness of their spring that's just around the corner, I exclaim over the profusion of camellias, roses, winter pansies, and blooming potted plants. I long to enter my garden in January and find enough to decorate even a petit four!*

GATHER YOUR MATERIALS

For a 9-inch round cake or torte with hard icing

10 very large ivy leaves (Increase the number if you have smaller ones.)

14 pansies

5 camellias, buds and fully opened flowers

9 ranunculus flowers

9-inch round cake or torte with a hard icing

Ribbon, ½ to 1 inch wide, 1-yard length (optional)

Candle and match

FLORAL CAKES PROJECT BASICS

FOR EACH ARRANGEMENT

Fresh flowers and leaves as specified in the project directions on pages 169–173

HOW TO BEGIN

1. Condition all fresh flowers and leaves in water for eight hours or overnight before using. Recut stems on an angle and place the flowers in a bucket of lukewarm water. The water level should be up to the flower heads. Add cut-flower preservative according to the package directions.

2. Check carefully for any signs of tiny creatures lurking between the petals, then rinse for dust. Use only flowers that have been grown without pesticides. This is not true of most florist flowers, so check before purchasing them for cake decorations.

3. Follow the instructions listed in the project directions on pages 169–173.

4. Decorate the cake just before serving to prevent the flowers and leaves from wilting. If the cake is already iced, it only takes a few minutes to add the floral trim.

NOTE: These flowers are for decoration only and must be removed when slicing the cake. Although pansies and roses are edible, ranunculus are definitely not, and it's best not to eat any flowers.

BACKYARD BITS
Serving the Cake

Before cutting the "Georgia in January" cake on page 168, untie the ribbon with a flourish, as you would a gift package. On this cake, only the pansies are edible. It's best to teach children never to eat flowers, berries, or leaves unless they are absolutely certain of their safety.

PUT THEM ALL TOGETHER

1 Begin by following the general instructions in the "Floral Cakes Project Basics," above.

2 When you are ready to decorate, set the ivy leaves around the cake plate and center the cake on top of the leaves.

3 Wrap the ribbon, if desired, around the cake and make a simple bow. Slip the pansy stems under the ribbon.

4 Cut off the stems of the other flowers. Singe the cut ends of the ranunculus blossoms over a candle flame to seal the stems (the sap can be irritating).

5 Pile the flowers in the center of the cake and sprinkle them generously around the bottom.

Spring in the Granite State

SPRING COMES LATE TO NEW HAMPSHIRE. *Lilacs, the state flower, don't bloom until mid-May. The wait is worth it when they perfume the air with their soft, sweet fragrance. Here I've used white lilacs to decorate a cake for a bridal shower, engagement party, or other affair of the heart and supplemented them with bits of sturdy foliage.*

171

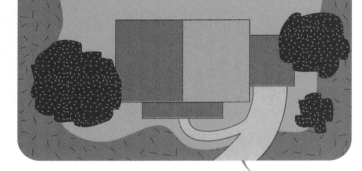

BACKYARD BITS

Culinary Mathematics

To make a heart-shaped cake, you have to remember your geometry. A 9-inch square has a larger area than a 9-inch circle. The two round cakes form two layers, so the square part of the cake is thinner. Baking, however, is not an exact science. Your goal is to have the square part of the cake match the height of the layered half-round cakes. If necessary, bake another half-recipe in the square pan. I generally prefer to fudge my way to perfect symmetry by slathering on an extra ½ inch of frosting.

GATHER YOUR MATERIALS

14 sprigs of lilac blossoms
 5 rhododendron leaves
12 stems of euonymus
   Double recipe of your favorite layer cake
   Double recipe of fluffy frosting, like marshmallow, meringue, or boiled icing
 1 cup of flaked coconut
 2 bows of organdy ribbon with long tails, 2 yards each (optional)

PUT THEM ALL TOGETHER

1 Begin by following the general instructions in the "Floral Cakes Project Basics" on page 170.

2 To form a large heart-shaped cake with no special pans or equipment, select your favorite layer-cake recipe. Divide the batter between two 9-inch round layer pans. Bake as directed, remove the cakes from the pans, and allow them to cool completely.

3 Make another recipe and bake it in a 9-inch-square pan. Remove it from the pan and allow it to cool. At this point, freeze the cakes until they're needed or continue to assemble and decorate.

4 Set the square cake on your tray or platter, turned so that it forms a diamond. Cut one round layer in half and position each half on one side of the diamond to form the heart shape.

5 Cut strips of waxed paper and slip them under the edges of the cake to catch the frosting splashes and coconut drips. Frost the top and sides.

6 Cut the second round cake in half and layer on top of the first halves. Finish frosting the cake and sprinkle with coconut.

7 Arrange several clusters of blossoms on the top of the cake and more blossoms and leaves around the base. Add the two ribbons, if desired.

Flower Power

Grow and Bake MY MOTHER WAS A BELIEVER IN THE SIMPLE THINGS IN LIFE: DAFFODILS IN SPRING-TIME, GERANIUMS IN SUMMER, BITTERSWEET FOR FALL, AND A WELL-BAKED BUTTER CAKE IN ALL SEASONS. THE CAKE, IF ICED, WOULD BE SIMPLY DECORATED WITH COCONUT, RAISINS, NUTS, OR A FEW FRESH STRAWBERRIES. A SIMPLE SWIRL IN THE FROSTING WITH A SPATULA OR AN ETCHING WITH THE TINES OF A FORK WAS AS ELABORATE AS SHE WAS PREPARED TO GO. THOUGH AS A CHILD I YEARNED FOR COLORED SPRINKLES, PIPED BLUE ROSES, AND MARZIPAN FRUITS PAINTED WITH A PINPOINT BRUSH, SHE REMAINED FIRM IN HER DIRECTION. SO WHILE I LEARNED TO BAKE AT A TENDER AGE, MY DECORATING SKILLS LAGGED FAR BEHIND.

WHEN MY THREE CHILDREN GREW UP AND MARRIED, I SOMEHOW EARNED THE HONOR AND PRIVILEGE OF HOSTING SMALL HOME WEDDINGS FOR EACH. I VOLUN-TEERED TO MAKE LUNCH AND BAKE FOR THESE SPECIAL OCCASIONS. BY THEN, I HAD STARTED IN MY FLOWER BUSINESS AND HAD AN ASSORTMENT OF FRESH FLOWERS AT HAND. I FOUND THAT SIMPLE BAKING, WITH THE ADDITION OF BEAUTIFUL ORGANICALLY GROWN BLOSSOMS, COULD MAKE ANY CAKE SPECIAL. NOW I THROW FRESH FLOWERS OR HERBS ON TOP OF ANYTHING I'M BAKING TO PRODUCE AN OCCASION.

Flower Dolls from the Farm

IN THE NOT-SO-OLDEN DAYS *when children made their toys and entertained themselves, girls in southern Illinois, like my friend Barbara Shaw, made dolls of hollyhock flowers and other blossoms. They made up plays starring their favorite creations and marched them along the porch rail. No matter that the dolls lasted one afternoon; the fun was in the making. Here flower dolls adorn a platter of cupcake cones for a birthday party or afternoon tea.*

GATHER YOUR MATERIALS

For each doll

3 or more assorted flower blossoms
   and buds like hollyhocks, marigolds,
   and bee balm
2 toothpicks

PUT THEM ALL TOGETHER

1 Invert the largest flower for the skirt, and use a large bud for the head and one or more blossoms for the headpiece or hat. Here I used a hollyhock for the skirt, a marigold bud for the head, and bee balm for the hat.

2 Break toothpicks in half and insert one end in the skirt and the other end in the head. Attach the head-dress in the same way. The style of the doll is limited only by your imagination.

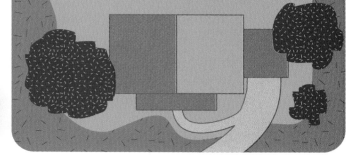

BACKYARD BITS
Ice-Cream Cone Cupcakes

To make the cupcakes shown with the hollyhock dolls, use your favorite cupcake recipe and ice-cream cones with a flat bottom. Don't use any cups that are cracked or have holes in them because the batter will just run out. Fill each cone two-thirds full with batter and stand it upright on a baking sheet. Bake at 350°F until the cake has risen and is brown on top. Use any leftover batter to make a small cake for another time. Decorate as desired. Here I used whipped cream, raspberries, and borage blossoms.

From Shore to Shore

WHEREVER THERE ARE SHELLS on a beach, there are scavengers collecting them, storing them in shoe boxes, and forgetting about them. Winnow through your collection to decorate these simple napkin rings and food covers. A set of either of them makes a unique hostess gift.

Ringing the Napkin

Cloth napkins add immeasurably to the grace of a table setting. Combine them with shell napkin rings for a touch of whimsy. Each napkin ring will be slightly different.

GATHER YOUR MATERIALS

For each napkin ring

> 2 or 3 small shells, preferably with holes
> Copper or gold 20-gauge wire
> White craft glue
> Pencil
> Wire cutters

FROM TOP TO BOTTOM: PRETTY FOR A PICNIC, RINGING THE NAPKIN, AND WEAVE A SPELL

Pretty for a Picnic

Picnics attract unwanted guests. Send them flying elsewhere when you keep the food protected with these simple-to-make picnic covers.

PUT THEM ALL TOGETHER

1 Cut off 5 feet of wire. Coil the wire tightly around the pencil, as shown below. Slide out the pencil and gently stretch the coil to 5 inches.

2 Form a circle with the coiled wire and wrap the ends around each other to hold in place.

3 If the shell has a hole, slip it on one end of the wire and glue it in place. Glue one or two more shells to the first shell. If none of the shells have holes, use glue to attach them to the wire. Allow to dry thoroughly before using.

GATHER YOUR MATERIALS

For each picnic cover

    4 or 5 small shells with holes
    8 to 10 beads, or more
    Old crocheted doily, fancy napkin, or
       linen handkerchief
    Needle and thread to match the doily

PUT THEM ALL TOGETHER

1 For a square doily, work the four corners; for round or other shape, work in five evenly spaced sections around the edge.

2 Thread the needle and knot the thread. Sew up from the "wrong" side of the doily. String on the beads, then the shell. Push the needle through the beads again, into the fabric where you started, and knot and cut the thread. Continue to do the other sections in the same way.

3 Place the picnic cover over a glass, a bowl, or a pitcher to protect your food and drink from insects and other unwanted guests.

Weave a Spell

Long, flat leaves, from grasslands or marshy areas, are a natural for the ancient craft of weaving. Because this woven table mat acts as the base for more elaborate objects, it is presented here in its most basic form. These directions work for place mats, table runners, or a covering for a small table. Adjust the number of leaves and the finished size to your own requirements.

GATHER YOUR MATERIALS

Cattail leaves (Here I used 76 leaves for a 40- by- 22 inch mat. You can substitute any flat leaf.)
Masking tape
Clippers
Glue gun and glue sticks

PUT THEM ALL TOGETHER

1 Find a large workplace where you can leave your mat undisturbed for a week or more. Sometimes the floor is best.

2 Separate the longest leaves and use them for the longest side if you're weaving a rectangular table cover. Use the shorter leaves for the shorter side. Tape the long leaves to the work surface vertically, as shown at right.

3 Take one of the shorter leaves and weave under and over near the taped edge, the way you made your pot holders as a child. Take the next leaf and weave over and under, as close as possible to the first woven element. Check your

weaving, straighten up the rows as necessary, and continue weaving until you have the approximate size mat you want. Do not trim or cut the edges yet. Let the mat dry in place.

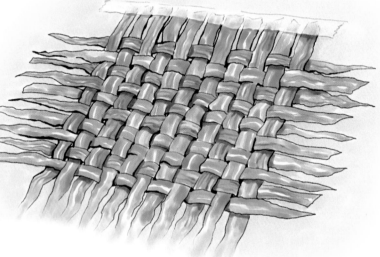

4 All leaves shrink as they dry. What looks like the perfect size when you make it may be two-thirds its size when it dries. Work on this project in three phases, allowing three or four days to elapse between each phase. Before beginning the second and third phases, move the leaves together, taking up the spaces left by shrinkage. Add more leaves until you reach the desired size mat.

5 After the third phase, when the leaves have dried, remove the tape, trim the ends of the leaves, and glue each leaf in place at both ends.

Jewelry & Wearables

Use dried flowers and pods to create fanciful jewelry and wearables. Enliven accessories with sturdy materials gathered from backyards and byways. Jazz up classic styles of dress with something unexpected from the garden. Compliments and smiles are guaranteed.

I photographed these mammoth live oak trees in Texas. Gather the acorns, leaves, and twigs to use for crafting.

A basket of buttercups, picked in my backyard, are bunched and ready for drying.

Live in a fourth floor walk up in New York City? That's no reason to deprive yourself of a garden.

*P*innacles

HAT PINS AND STICKPINS *are enjoying a resurgence of favor.*
Young women wear hat pins to decorate a turned up brim,
never guessing that they once were functional, securing hats to long
tresses. Other women adorn lapels of suits with stickpins to lighten
the look. Here are some custom-made pins, each featuring a
different natural material from around the country.

FROM LEFT TO RIGHT: LARGE POPPY POD WITH TASSEL, SMALL CHESTNUT WITH
BEADS, JOB'S-TEARS POD WITH SILVER TASSEL, ORIENTAL NIGELLA POD WITH GOLD
BUTTON, LIVE OAK ACORN WITH GOLD RIBBON, EUCALYPTUS POD WITH GOLD CORD,
STRAWFLOWER WITH BEADS, AND SMALL POPPY POD WITH ANTIQUE BEAD

GATHER YOUR MATERIALS

For each pin

Pod, nut, or flower (Here I used large and small poppy pods, an oriental nigella pod, and a strawflower from my garden in Pennsylvania; a live oak acorn from Texas; a Job's-tears pod from Hawaii; a chestnut from Delaware; and a eucalyptus pod from California.)

5-inch stickpin jewelry finding in silver or gold or 6-inch hat pin finding in silver or gold (This is available from a jewelry or craft supply store.)

Assortment of new and old beads, buttons, tassels, narrow ribbon, and cording

Crimp (the tiny last bead on the pin to help hold the others in place)

Clutch (the stopper at the bottom of the pin that keeps you from poking yourself)

Tube of glue for metal, like Bond 527

Toothpick

Needle-nose pliers

Small scissors

PUT THEM ALL TOGETHER

1 Take a stickpin finding and slide the beads on in the order you prefer. I often start with a small round or tear-shaped bead for the top. When wearing a pin, people usually push it through their clothing by applying pressure on the top bead. Protect your flower or pod by having a hard bead at the top.

2 All the beads must be glued in place one by one. With the toothpick, put glue on the pin at the top. Slide on the top bead and twirl it around so the inside of the bead gets coated with glue. Continue to put glue on the pin and twirl on a bead until the design is complete. Remove any excess glue with another toothpick as you add the beads.

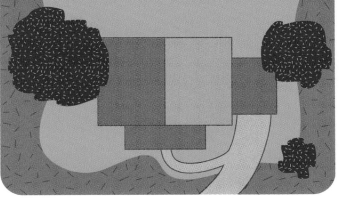

BACKYARD BITS
Collecting Ornamental Beads

You may have a few beads roaming around your jewelry box that have come off of yesterday's jewels. Friends will make contributions of their own, too, especially if they anticipate receiving one of your lovely creations as an exchange. You can find inexpensive costume jewelry at yard sales that can be cut apart for beads. Look for necklaces with both small and large beads in several different colors. Take a stickpin with you when you go searching to make sure the bead hole is the right size. Fish through your button box for small gold, silver, and rhinestone buttons with shanks. To buy beads, examine the selections in craft stores or at the mail-order sources listed on page 202, but beware: it's almost impossible not to overbuy. Don't say I didn't warn you.

3 The last bead is a tiny crimp. Put a bit of glue on the pin, slide on the crimp and squeeze it tightly with the pliers. The crimp will help hold the beads in place, but the glue is the main fixative.

New Mexican Cowgirls

WHILE I WAS VISITING MY FRIEND *Frances White in Santa Fe, I was persuaded to buy this red cowboy hat, while she bought the more conservative black one. To make them more outrageous, I trimmed my hat with a band of cayenne peppers and dried chamiza, which bursts into brilliant gold in the late New Mexican summer, and trimmed Frances's hat with a strand of yellow Thai peppers interspersed with small black ones.*

GATHER YOUR MATERIALS

For each hat

Small fresh peppers, enough to string around the crown of a hat (Here I used 94 cayenne peppers for the red hat and 88 Thai peppers for the black hat.)
Additional bits of dried flowers (optional) (Here I used chamiza.)
Dental floss or monofilament fishing line
Needle
Scissors
Glue gun and glue sticks

PUT THEM ALL TOGETHER

1 Cut off a piece of dental floss or fishing line, long enough to double and go around the crown of the hat, plus an extra foot.

2 Thread the needle with the doubled floss, knot the end, and string the fresh peppers. Since the peppers shrink by about 25 percent when they dry, string on more than you think you need. It's easier to take off the extras later rather than add them. Be sure to keep your fingers away from your eyes, nose, and mouth during the process or you'll get a hot surprise.

3 Hang the string in a warm spot until the peppers are dry. Glue flower bits onto the dried peppers, as desired.

4 Gently push the peppers together on the thread to take up the shrinkage that occurred during the drying process.

5 Tie the strand around the crown of the hat and cut off the extra thread. It is completely removable if you want to wear the hat without the peppers and can be replaced easily when you are feeling adventurous.

High Fashion from the Big Apple

NEW YORK CITY PROCLAIMS ITSELF BOTH *the World Capital and the Fashion Capital of the United States. It's true that you see some very unusual fashion statements on the city streets. While this shoe is no longer a "wearable," it once danced at parties and weddings on the foot of Dolores Delin of Pottsville, Pennsylvania. Display this fanciful footwear on a side table, in a guest room, or anywhere you want to be amused.*

GATHER YOUR MATERIALS

89 pressed buttercups (See "Seven Methods of Preserving Flowers and Herbs" on page 194 for more information.)

14 acorn caps (You can substitute dried rosebuds.)

5 peacock feathers

Queen-Anne's-lace flower, pressed

Maple-seed capsules

High-heeled shoe from attic, flea market, or second-hand shop

Matte black spray paint

White craft glue

Toothpick

Scissors

PUT THEM ALL TOGETHER

1 Spray paint the shoe black inside and out, with one or two coats of paint in a well-ventilated area and set it aside to dry.

2 Think through your design before you start; the more fanciful the arrangement is, the better. All the materials are glued onto the shoe beginning with the smaller elements.

3 Use the toothpick as a glue spreader. To glue on small, delicate materials like the pressed buttercups, spread the glue on the shoe surface and cover it with the flowers. For larger elements like the acorn caps, spread the glue on each piece and set in place.

4 Cut the pieces as necessary to fit the shoe surface and your design. For example, I left the peacock "eyes" on the sides of the shoe their natural size, but trimmed the others to fit the instep.

BACKYARD BITS
Cityscapes

As I walk around New York City, I stoop to gather pods that the street trees shed. Acorns, locust pods, horse chestnuts, and maple-seed capsules are all fair game. (We used to call these capsules nosies, the unenlightened called them helicopters.) The park system and the sidewalk cracks offer up wildflowers and grasses that are suitable for pressing and drying. Observe local laws and don't pick anything that is endangered.

Peacocks strut in the gardens of the Cathedral of St. John the Divine on 110th Street and Broadway. Although I can't gather the molting feathers, the image of the elegant birds and the magnificent cathedral stays with me when I later purchase my feathers in a craft shop. Follow my example and gather what you can from your own backyard, then fill in with purchased materials from your local craft store or florist.

Southern Treasures

THESE ELEGANT TREASURES *had humble beginnings as pods and seeds of common plants found throughout the South. Gather materials from your neck of the woods to create your own indigenous accessories.*

Chained to Kentucky

The Kentucky coffee tree produces lustrous brown leathery pods that drop in the spring. Where some see a cleanup nuisance, I see a source of durable beads. Nestled inside each pod amid some sticky matter are two to four hard brown seeds. The Manual of Woody Landscape Plants, the official tree bible for landscapers, states that the seeds were used by the early settlers as a coffee substitute. They also report that "the seeds are great fun to throw and hit with a baseball bat." Be that as it may, I recommend a necklace instead.

GATHER YOUR MATERIALS

40 to 48 washed Kentucky coffee tree seeds
24-gauge copper or gold wire
Copper or gold-tone pull chain, 5-foot length (This is available by the foot from hardware stores.)
Wire clippers
Needle-nose pliers
Ruler

BACKYARD BITS
Hard Seed to Crack

I gathered Kentucky coffee tree seeds in the spring. My first design involved drilling a hole in the seed to make a bead, but I found it was almost impossible. These are the hardest seeds I have ever worked with, hence the necessity for the wrapping technique. When the seeds first form in the fall, the shell may be softer and easier to pierce. However, very few pods drop from the trees then, so there might not be enough to gather.

FROM TOP TO BOTTOM: OKRA TRANSFORMED, CHAINED TO KENTUCKY

PUT THEM ALL TOGETHER

1 For each seed, cut an 18-inch length of wire. Wrap the seed with the wire, wrapping in all directions and weaving the wire randomly in and out to keep it secure. Leave ¼ inch of wire on the end and form a hook with the pliers.

2 When all the seeds are wrapped with the wire, space them evenly along the length of the chain. Measure the distance between each to keep them even as you work.

3 To attach a seed to the chain, place the hook between two tiny balls of the chain, and squeeze the hook with the pliers to tighten.

Okra Transformed

Louisiana gumbo is a treat for some, while others shudder at the thought of the soup, thickened with gelatinous okra. Here dried okra pods and seeds transform a ribbon into a simple decoration for a hair clasp. It's funky enough to wear for the Mardi Gras and elegant enough for a cotillion.

GATHER YOUR MATERIALS

38 okra seeds
2 small dried okra pods
Ribbon with fancy-trim edges,
   1½ inches wide, 20-inch length
Hair clasp
White craft glue
Toothpick

BACKYARD BITS
Ribbon Bows

For the "Okra Transformed" hair clip, I tied the ribbon in a traditional bow, but any type of bow will work. Try a more ornate bow with six loops for a dressier occasion, or one with longer tails for a child with long hair. Just remember to adjust the amount of ribbon and okra seeds you need accordingly.

BACKYARD BITS

For Crafting and Cooking

Okra is closely related to the tropical flower hibiscus, which explains the large yellow flowers the plant produces. It is a heat-loving plant with heart-shaped leaves and a woody stem. Okra is undemanding to grow but needs a long growing season. If you live in the North, look for varieties that specify "short-season cultivar." These types require approximately seven to nine weeks to mature. After the flowers bloom, green pods will form; let them mature until they turn beige and dry on the stem. Then you can pick them and use them for any decorative purpose. Dried okra pods, often with the seeds still inside, are available at good dried flower marts. You can also purchase a packet of seeds separately from most seed catalogs and garden centers. Fresh okra has long been a staple of southern cooking. Add the vegetable in the green stage to soups and stews or coat it with cornmeal and fry.

PUT THEM ALL TOGETHER

1 Tie a simple bow with the ribbon and glue it to the back of the hair clasp. Wait for the glue to dry before proceeding to the next step.

2 Use the toothpick to dab glue on the okra seeds, and place the seeds next to the trim along one edge of the ribbon, as shown in the photo on the opposite page.

3 With your fingernails, gently split apart the pods along the natural ridges, and open them up like a flower. Glue the pods to the center of the bow, with the pearly inside showing. If the pods break apart in the process, glue the pieces to the center of the bow as well.

Running Wild

VARIOUS FORMS OF YUCCA *grow wild in the dry heat of the Southwest. Gardeners in Zones 5 through 11 plant the hardy perennial for its stately form in the bloom and pod stages. The dried pods resemble peanuts and are tough enough to string as beads for wearing. Many thanks to Elke Kuhn Moore, who taught me this technique and provided the bobbins.*

GATHER YOUR MATERIALS

4 yucca pods (You can substitute any sturdy pod for the yucca, such as fennel or poppy pods.)

15 poppy pods

2 oriental fennel pods

12 beads with holes large enough to slip over the wire

28 bobbins with thread (You can substitute other beads.)

3 to 5 buttons with shanks

9 bobby pins, each 3 inches long

16- or 18-gauge copper wire, 18-inch length

24 pieces of ribbon, ¹⁄₁₆ to 2 inches
   wide, 8-inch lengths (You can
   substitute narrow cord.)
Piece of ribbon, ⅜ inch wide,
   18-inch length
Masking tape
White craft glue
Carpet needle, or other needle
   with a large eye
Scissors
Toothpick
Needle-nose pliers
Wire cutter

PUT THEM ALL TOGETHER

1 This looks complicated but it's fairly easy
to do if you plan in advance. Horizontal
elements are strung from the copper wire
that forms the necklace. Bobby pins dangle
down from the copper wire and hold the
vertical elements. Use the long ribbon to
tie the ends of the wire together at the
back of the neck, as shown below.

2 Poke holes in the pods with the
needle in order to slip them on
the wire or bobby pin.

3 Lay out the elements for the copper
wire. Here I have used from left to
center: bead, yucca, bead, bead, bobbin,
bobbin, bead, bead, bobbin, bobbin, yucca,
bead. The other side repeats the pattern
from the right to the center. Use any
arrangement you wish.

4 When you are satisfied with the
design, string the elements onto the
wire. Beads slip off while you work, so
stick a wad of tape on one end as a tempo-
rary protective measure.

5 Slip the bobby pins over the wire
between the beads in an even pattern,
making sure one bobby pin is in the center
of the necklace. Slide pods, buttons, and
bobbins onto the bobby pin. Squeeze the
pin together to slip the elements on; when
it's released, it will hold them in place.
Tie on two or three pieces of ribbon at
intervals along each bobby pin and trim
the ends of the ribbon to the desired
lengths.

6 Thread the needle with very thin
ribbon or cord, and draw it through a
pod. Knot one end and tie the other to the
bobby pin, letting the pod dangle.

7 To keep the ribbon from fraying,
spread a small amount of white glue
along the cut edges with the toothpick.

8 Remove the tape from both ends
of the copper wire. With the needle-
nose pliers, turn one end into a small
closed loop. Cut any excess wire from
the other end and make another loop.

9 Thread the 18-inch length of ribbon
through both loops. To wear, slip it
over your head and tie the ends in a bow.

Seven Methods of Preserving Flowers and Herbs

IF YOU HAVE *a limited repertoire of plant preserving skills, you may want to give some of these methods a try. Keep in mind that not every flower and herb can be dried by the same method, so I've given you some guidance on which methods will work best with certain plant materials. Don't be afraid to experiment. Some of my best dried creations arose from an afternoon that started off with my thinking, "I'll just give this a try...."*

AIR DRYING

Bunch together plant materials like flowers, herbs, and corn leaves with a rubber band and hang them upside down from a wire, line, or hook. The atmosphere where they're hung should be warm, dark, and dry. Each house or apartment is different, but if you have an attic, that is likely to be a good spot.

There is no need to strip the leaves from flowers before you air-dry them. In fact, most will look more natural if you dry them with the leaves on. Materials will shrink as they dry, so the roses you started with will look about half the size

Flower Power

when they're dried. If you expect that to happen, you won't be displeased.

Air-dry whole artichokes and small hot peppers from the garden or supermarket by leaving them on a cookie rack in a warm, dark, and dry place.

Oven Dehydrating

Use your oven as a dehydrator for fruits and large flowers. A very slow oven set at 140° to 200°F, with the exhaust fan on, removes excess humidity as the materials dry. Check frequently for dryness and color. The petals dry first and will feel crispy. The fleshy part at the top of the stem dries last. The length of time depends on the size and fleshiness of the fruits or flowers and the amount you dry at one time. A single flower will dry faster than an ovenful of flowers.

Place larger flowers, like sunflowers and peonies, directly on the oven rack; for smaller flowers lay a piece of window screening over the rack so they won't fall between the wires. The smaller the flowers, the lower the oven temperature should be. Peonies will take about 2 to 3 hours, while sunflowers will take over 10 hours to dry. Be sure to remove the flowers from the oven before they begin to brown.

To dehydrate fruits like citrus or pomegranate slices, cut the fruit into ¼-inch slices. Pat the slices dry with a paper towel and place them on a cookie sheet covered with waxed paper. Dehydrate the fruit for about 2 hours, turning the pieces once. If the paper gets too brown from baking juices, reline the cookie sheet with clean waxed paper before turning the slices.

For apple slices follow the same directions but soak them first for one hour in a quart of water mixed with 3 tablespoons of salt and 2 tablespoons of lemon juice. Pat the slices dry before dehydrating.

If you live in a humid climate, large hot peppers or long sweet peppers are too fleshy to air-dry. Dehydrate them in an oven (or food dehydrator) on a cookie sheet as described above, but slit one side to allow the steam to escape. Dry the peppers for 8 to 10 hours in a slow oven; if the temperature is too high, you will have roasted peppers.

To dry whole lemons, limes, or small oranges, select well-colored fruit with a thick rind that's not too juicy, just the opposite of your choice for eating. Slit the rind vertically with a paring knife, cutting into the flesh slightly and stopping before you reach the end, as shown below. Make six or eight cuts in the same way. Dry for 6 to 10 hours.

Remove all fruits and vegetables from the oven before they begin to brown, and let them continue to air-dry slowly in a warm spot, like on top of your refrigerator. I put mine under a freestanding radiator. Spray dried fruits and vegetables with polyurethane spray, shellac, or varnish to prevent insect attacks.

BACKYARD BITS
UNDER THE RUG

You don't need to invest in fancy equipment to dry flowers and leaves. All of the pressed fern leaves that I used in the projects in this book were dried under my dining room rug. I made a sandwich of newspapers, laid the leaves in between, then slid the paper under the pad and rug. The fern dried within a week.

USING A FOOD DEHYDRATOR

All food dehydrators that I've seen have shallow trays. You can stack the trays to dry more materials simultaneously, but there is not enough depth for really thick material. Small flowers and fruit slices work best. The instructions that come with your dehydrator may help, but most don't give instructions for drying flowers.

Cut off the stems of roses, marigolds, zinnias, dahlias, bachelor's buttons, or other flowers and place them face down on the dehydrating tray. You can crowd them a little because the flowers will shrink one-third to one-half as they dry. Follow the recommended settings on your machine. Remember that petals dry first, possibly within an hour, but the thick part at the base of the stem might not be dry for 10 hours or more. This is not an exact science, so check the base for dryness before removing the flowers. Store them in an air-tight container until ready for use.

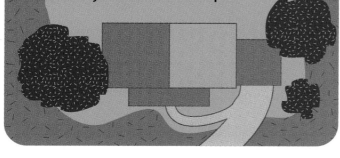

Use only perfect flowers and leaves in the prime of life, including buds, just-opened flowers, grasses, and weeds, all gathered when the dew or rain has evaporated. Don't crowd the flowers in the press. As the flowers dry, they shrink, loosening the press and diminishing contact. Retighten the press every day until it can no longer be tightened.

Change absorbent paper after three days by carefully removing the flowers with tweezers or the flat edge of a paring knife and repositioning them on dry paper. If using a telephone book, switch to another book at this point. This step reduces mildewing and browning of the flowers as they dry.

PRESSING

Pressing is an easy and attractive way to preserve the beauty of many kinds of leaves and flowers. Pressed flowers need a warm, dry atmosphere to retain their vibrant colors. They must be heavily weighted in order to dry flat and smooth. For a few pieces, a telephone book will suffice. But if you have more, a flower press is most practical.

You can either purchase a flower press or make one of scrap lumber. To make one, use two rectangular pieces of plywood and drill a hole in each corner. Place the pieces together and insert a bolt with wing nut into each hole. Use these to tighten your press.

Press flowers between layers of absorbent paper, like blotter paper or blank newsprint. Beware of colored or inky papers that may bleed onto the flowers when damp, and embossed papers, like napkins and paper towels, that will impress little designs into the flowers. Test printed newspaper to see that it doesn't bleed.

IRONING

Iron leaves and flowers when you need pressed materials in a desperate hurry. Set the iron on medium heat and put a hard surface, such as a wood cutting board, on the ironing board. On top of this, place two or three layers of newspaper, then a single layer of leaves or flowers you need to press.

Flower Power

Cover the leaves of the flowers with two or three more layers of newspaper. Now press this stack with the iron, constantly keeping it in motion so there is no scorching. After about 10 minutes, carefully turn over the whole pile and iron on the reverse side. Check in 5 minutes to see if the material is completely dried and flat; if not, continue for another short time. The length of time for ironing depends on the thickness and water content of the materials. Thin leaves like fern and bracts like bougainvillea are best.

DRYING IN SILICA GEL

Silica gel is a desiccant that quickly removes moisture from flowers and leaves, allowing them to retain their wonderful colors, and if you are careful, their original shape. For some flowers, like lilies, orchids, dogwood, tulips, and iris, it is the preferred method of home drying.

Each package of silica gel comes with complete instructions. The process involves burying the plant material by pouring a layer of silica at the bottom of a cookie tin, Tupperware, or other airtight container, placing the flower on top (with the stem cut short), and pouring the silica all around the outside of the flower. When it begins to form a mound that will support the petals and prevent them from flattening, gently cover the flower with another inch of silica.

It's best to wear a dust mask if you will be doing a lot of drying with silica gel. In one to two weeks, depending on the size and moisture content of the flowers, they will be dry. Gently pour off the silica into another container, exposing the flowers. Most flowers dried this way should be sprayed with a lacquer spray, like petal sealer, or hair spray to prevent reabsorption of moisture.

WAXING

Waxing fresh fruits and flowers with paraffin creates an old-world look and prolongs the life of the material. For most fresh items, it is not a permanent fix. Wax dried flowers and leaves in the same way to help preserve the color and create a different texture.

Paraffin is highly flammable so you must use a double boiler to heat it. Put the paraffin in a coffee can and set it in a pot of water, no higher than halfway up the can. This is a homemade double boiler. Allow the water to come to a boil and immediately decrease the heat to a

Flower Power

Shape Yes, Color No BECAUSE SO MANY PEOPLE HAVE SUGGESTED DESICCANTS OTHER THAN SILICA GEL, I RECENTLY TRIED BURYING FLOWERS IN FOUR OTHER MEDIA: TWO BRANDS OF CAT LITTER, CORNMEAL, AND OATS. ONE BRAND OF LITTER HAD SMALL GRANULES AND ONE HAD LARGER GRANULES. I EXPERIMENTED WITH PINK ROSES, WHITE ASIATIC LILIES, AND MUMS. FORGET THE OATS—THE RESULTS WERE UNPLEASANT! THE CORNMEAL AND TWO KINDS OF LITTER GAVE SIMILAR RESULTS—GOOD RETENTION OF SHAPE BUT ONLY FAIR RETENTION OF COLOR. IN ADDITION, THE LITTER OVERPOWERED ME WITH THE AROMA OF A PERFUME ADDITIVE. SO I'LL STICK TO SILICA GEL, USING A DUST MASK, WHEN I NEED PERFECTION IN DRYING.

low setting. You want to melt all the paraffin but not have it very hot.

Dip clean, dry fruit or flowers in paraffin, covering all areas including the stem if any. I prefer to dip in two stages, first one half then the other, using just my fingers. Use tongs to hold your material if that is more to your liking.

Hold the dipped piece over the can and gently shake off excess wax until it stops dripping. Set the piece on a plate or sheet of waxed paper to harden; stand stems in dry floral foam to hold upright. Use immediately in an arrangement, or store for several days in an open container.

For more details on drying flowers and herbs, see my book *Flower Crafts: A Step-by-Step Guide to Growing, Drying, and Decorating with Flowers.* (See "Suggested Reading" on the opposite page.)

Suggested Reading

Dirr, Michael A. *Manual of Woody Landscape Plants: Their Identification, Ornamental Characteristics, Culture, Propagation and Uses.* Champaign, IL: Stipes Publishing Company, 1977.

Embertson, Jane. *Pods, Wildflowers and Weeds.* New York: Simon & Schuster, 1980.

Halfacre, R. Gordon and Shawncroft, Anne R. *Landscaping Plants of the Southeast.* Raleigh, NC: Sparks Press, 1989.

Niering, William A. and Olmstead, Nancy C. *Audubon Society Field Guide to North American Wildflowers, Eastern Region.* New York: Alfred A. Knopf, 1995.

Platt, Ellen Spector. *Flower Crafts: A Step-by-step Guide to Growing, Drying and Decorating with Flowers.* Emmaus, PA: Rodale Press, 1993.

——— *How to Profit from Flower & Herb Crafts.* Mechanicsburg, PA: Stackpole Books, 1996.

——— *The Ultimate Wreath Book: Hundreds of Beautiful Wreaths to Make from Natural Materials.* Emmaus, PA: Rodale Press, 1995.

——— *Wreaths, Arrangements & Basket Decorations: Using Flowers, Foliage, Herbs and Grasses to Make Colorful Crafts.* Emmaus, PA: Rodale Press, 1994.

Rosenfeld, Lois G. *The Garden Tourist: A Guide to Garden Tours, Garden Days, Shows and Special Events.* New York: Garden Tourist Press, new edition yearly.

Spellenberg, Richard. *Audubon Society Field Guide to North American Wildflowers, Western Region.* New York: Alfred A. Knopf, 1995.

Sources

SUPPLIES

Diane Arnold
261 East Genesee
Auburn, NY 13021
(315) 252-6780
★ Cakes

Bead Warehouse
55 San Remo Drive
South Burlington, VT 05403
(800) 736-0781
★ Full-color, mail-order catalog
of beads and jewelry supplies

Harvest Naturals
Route 1, Box 245
Walnut Ridge, AK 72476
(501) 892-5601
★ Decorative wheat

Mark Hopkins
82 N. State Street
Concord, NH 03301
(603) 228-5446
★ Miniature furniture reproductions
and custom furniture designs

Loose Ends Paper Company
P.O. Box 20310
Salem, OR 97307
(503) 390-7457
★ Unique paper and ribbon

M & J Trimming
1008 Sixth Avenue
New York, NY 10018
(212) 391-9072
★ Beads, buttons, ribbon, braid, lace,
feathers, and decorative findings

M. T. Nest
Michael A. Trusky & Jeff Hubler
R. D. 1, Box 63 C
Hegins, PA 17938
(717) 682-8548
★ Home-grown ostrich eggs;
mail-order available

Maxilla & Mandible
451 Columbus Avenue
New York, NY 10024
(212) 724-6173
★ A natural history and science
emporium offering shells,
fossils, and minerals

Salt Box Frames
Pamela Young
511 Arrowhead Trail
Sinking Spring, PA 19608
(618) 678-6710
★ Faux-finish frames and graining
with comb and feather designs

Ed Ware
P.O. Box 795
San Antonio, TX 78293
 ★ Collected natural materials from
 South Texas; mail-order available

Windflower Farms, Inc.
40 Island Road
White Swan, WA 98952-9752
(509) 848-2490; fax (509) 848-2491
 ★ Preserved hops

SEEDS

Bountiful Gardens
18001 Shafer Ranch Road
Willits, CA 95490
(707) 459-6410

W. Atlee Burpee & Company
300 Park Avenue
Warminster, PA 18974
(800) 333-5808

The Cook's Garden
P.O. Box 535
Londonderry, VT 05148
(802) 824-3400

Johnny's Selected Seeds
Foss Hill Road
Albion, ME 04910
(207) 437-4357

Nichols Garden Nursery
1190 N. Pacific Highway
Albany, OR 97321
(541) 928-9280

Park Seed Company
Cokesbury Road
Greenwood, SC 29647
(800) 845-3369

Shepherd's Garden Seeds
30 Irene Street
Torrington, CT 06790
(806) 482-3638

Thompson & Morgan, Inc.
P.O. Box 1308
Jackson, NJ 08527
(800) 274-7333

USDA Plant Hardiness Zone Map

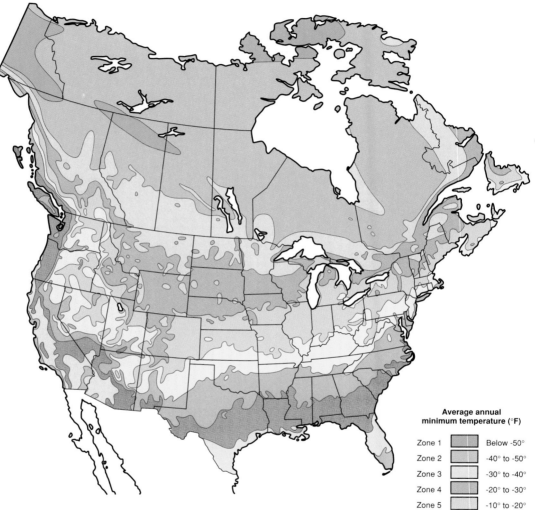

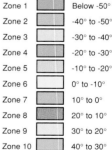

Average annual minimum temperature (°F)

Zone 1		Below -50°
Zone 2		-40° to -50°
Zone 3		-30° to -40°
Zone 4		-20° to -30°
Zone 5		-10° to -20°
Zone 6		0° to -10°
Zone 7		10° to 0°
Zone 8		20° to 10°
Zone 9		30° to 20°
Zone 10		40° to 30°

This map was revised in 1990 to reflect the original USDA map, done in 1965. It is now recognized as the best estimator of minimum temperatures available. Look at the map to find your area, then match its pattern to the key on the right. When you've found your pattern, the key will tell you what hardiness zone you live in. Remember that the map is a general guide; your particular conditions may vary.

Index

Note: Page references in **boldface** indicate photographs.
References in *italic* indicate illustrations.

Roses
  arrangements of, 44, **45, 68,**
    69
  collage of, 128, **129**
  harvesting, 196

S

Salal (lemon leaf), **13,** 14–15
Salsify (goatsbeard), **76,** 77
Scotch broom, **52–53,** 53–54
Seashells
  in collage, 130–31, **130–31**
  in market tray arrangement,
    58–60, **58–59, 60**
  on napkin rings, 176–78,
    176–77, 178
Sedum, **74,** 75
Seed pods, **182**
  on hair clasp, 190–91, **190**
  in necklace, 191–93, **192**
  on papier-mâché bottles,
    137, 139, **139**
Seed sources, 203
Silica gel, 198, 199
Stickpins, 182–83, **182**
Strawflowers
  harvesting, 196
  on hat pins or stickpins, **182**
  in market tray arrangement,
    62, 63
Sugar cane, 110–12, **110–11**
Sumac
  topiary, 81, **81**
  wreath, 6, *6,* **7**
Sunflowers, *23*
  arrangement of, 72, **73**
  drying, 196
  in wreath, 22–23, **22**
Supply sources, 202–203
Swags
  apple and lemon leaf,
    13–15, **13,** *15*

blueberry and raspberry,
    24–26, **25**
eucalyptus, 2–5, **2–3,** *4*
planning, 26
Texas foliage, 120–21, **120,**
    121

T

Table decorations. *See* Cake decorations; Napkin rings; Table
  mat
Table mat, **176–77,** 179, **179,** *179*
Table runner, 179, **179,** *179*
Thanksgiving mantel arrangement, 88–89, **88–89**
Tomato cage collage, **148,**
  149–151, *150*
Topiaries
  boxwood Christmas tree,
    116, 117, *117*
  larkspur, 78, **79**
  pressed leaf, 81, **81**
  project basics, 80, *80*
Twigs
  vases made of, 52–55,
    52–53, *54,* **55**
  wreath base made of, 23, *23*

V

Vases, twig, 52–55, **52–53,** *54,*
  55

W

Wall decorations. *See* Swags;
  Wallhangings; Wreaths
Wallhangings
  apple and lemon leaf, **13,**
    14–15

bamboo, **8,** 9
birch twig, 10, **10**
pussy willow, 12, **12**
shapes of, 5
weaving technique for, 11, *11*
Waxing fruit, flowers and leaves,
  18, 39, 199–200, *200*
Weaving
  in bamboo wallhanging, **8,** 9
  in birch twig wallhanging,
    10, **10**
  in cat tail table mat, **176–77,**
    179, **179,** *179*
  in pussy willow wall-
    hanging, 12, **12**
  techniques for, 11, *11,* 179,
    179
Weeping willow, **30**
  in centerpiece, 32–35, **32–33**
  napkin rings, 35
Wheat stems, **137,** 141, **141**
Willow. *See* Fan-tail willow;
  Weeping willow
Wreaths. *See also* Swags
  corn, 22–23, **22**
  devil's claw, 118, *118,* **119**
  hanger for, 18
  magnolia, 27–29, **27,** *28, 29*
  planning, 26
  shapes of, 5
  sumac, 6, *6,* **7**
  table, **16,** 17–18
  twig base for, 23, *23*
  wire base for, 28, *28*

Y

Yucca pods, 192–93, **192**

Z

Zinnias, 196